PICKING ON MEN

The First Honest
Collection
of Quotations
About Men

PICKING ON MEN

The First Honest Collection of Quotations About Men

Judy Allen

FAWCETT GOLD MEDAL • NEW YORK

Contents

2 MEN, Stages in Life of

Introduction

Everyone has heard at least one mother-in-law joke, but how many can remember a father-in-law joke? The phrase 'woman driver' raises a laugh before any more is added, but no one has much to say about male drivers. Current collections of quotations tend to include whole sections of disparaging remarks about women, but very few about men. Here is a collection to help to redress the balance.

It might be argued that in one or two cases the words 'man' or 'men' actually mean 'mankind' and therefore include women. However, in general it is men—that is, males—who choose to call the whole of humanity 'man', and therefore they must resign themselves to being struck by a backlash, hoist with their own petard(s).

> Male arrogance is embedded in our language . . . It is a convention of the English language to describe a person of undetermined sex as male; inevitably, though, a whole set of meanings accompany the use of the masculine pronoun in this way—without realizing it, we place in our minds a mental picture of a man, however vaguely, and give him a male persona.
>
> **Andrew Goodman,** *A Book About Men*
> (Andrew Goodman and Patricia Welby)

PICKING ON MEN

A man never begins by presenting himself as an individual of a certain sex; it goes without saying that he is a man . . . In actuality the relation of the two sexes is not quite like that of two electrical poles, for man represents both the positive and the neutral, as is dictated by the common use of *man* to designate human beings in general; whereas woman represents only the negative, defined by limiting criteria, without reciprocity.

Simone de Beauvoir, *The Second Sex*

(A person is) a male person, including an Indian and excluding a person of Mongolian or Chinese race.

Canada Franchise Act, 1885

In men this blunder still you find—
All think their little set mankind.

Hannah More, *Florio and His Friends*

. . . just as for the ancients there was an absolute vertical with reference to which the oblique was defined, so there is an absolute human type, the masculine . . . Thus humanity is male and man defines woman not in herself but as relative to him; she is not regarded as an autonomous being.

Simone de Beauvoir, *The Second Sex*

The collected quotations have been grouped in sections to make them more accessible. Quite a few of them, of course, seemed to fit as well into one section as into another—so the arrangement is fairly arbitrary, but with a bit of luck it should still help you to locate a particular comment. Unless, that is, you know who said it, in which case there is the index. The compiler and the editor don't necessarily agree with the sentiments of every single one of the quotations which follow—but we had a lot of fun reading them.

Finally, this book is not complete. There are more quotes out there somewhere. If you know of something that's missing, please send it in for inclusion in any future edition. Many thanks.

1

MEN

Aspects of

MEN

Definitions of

What would ye, ladies? It was ever thus.
Men are unwise and curiously planned.

James Elroy Flecker

Men are like eggs—they're fresh, rotten or hard-boiled.

Jacob M. Braude, quoted in *Speaker's
Encyclopaedia*, Prentice-Hall

Most men are like eggs, too full of themselves to hold anything
else.

Josh Billings, quoted in *The Book of
Unusual Quotations* (Rudolph Flesch), Cassell

The average man: one who thinks he isn't.

Jacob M. Braude, quoted in *Speaker's
Encyclopaedia*, Prentice-Hall

Male, n. A member of the unconsidered, or negligible sex. The
male of the human race is commonly known (to the female) as
Mere Man. The genus has two varieties: good providers and bad
providers.

Ambrose Bierce, *The Devil's Dictionary*, Penguin

PICKING ON MEN

Man is the second strongest sex in the world.

Philip Barry, quoted in *Bartlett's Unfamiliar Quotations* (Leonard Louis Levinson)

Most men are bad.

Bias of Prierie

Man was created a little lower than the angels, and he has been getting a little lower ever since.

Josh Billings, quoted in *Bartlett's Unfamiliar Quotations* (Leonard Louis Levinson)

Every man is as God hath made him, and sometimes a great deal worse.

Cervantes, *Don Quixote*

The male is a domestic animal which, if treated with firmness and kindness, can be trained to do most things.

Jilly Cooper, *Cosmopolitan*, October 1972

Men are like cellophane—transparent but hard to remove once you get wrapped up in them.

Jacob M. Braude, quoted in *Speaker's Encyclopaedia*, Prentice-Hall

Men are but children of a larger growth.

John Dryden, quoted in *Quotations for Our Time* (Dr. Laurence Peter)

Man is nature's sole mistake.

W.S. Gilbert, *Princess Ida*

Man—a reasoning rather than a reasonable animal.

Alexander Hamilton, quoted in *Peter's Quotations* (Dr. Laurence Peter), Morrow

MEN, Definitions of

Man is creation's masterpiece; but who says so?

Elbert Hubbard, quoted in *Peter's Quotations* (Dr. Laurence Peter), Morrow

Man is an intelligence in servitude to his organs.

Aldous Huxley, *Theme and Variations*

Man is a blind, witless, low-brow, anthropocentric clod who inflicts lesions on the earth.

Ian McHarg, quoted in *Quotations for Our Time* (Dr. Laurence Peter)

Men are nicotine-soaked, beer-besmeared, whisky-greased, red-eyed devils.

Carry Nation

Mammal embryos, deprived of any input of either male or female hormones, always develop as structurally female. Man, in other words, is an afterthought of creation: he is simply a modification of the female.

Deborah Moggach, reviewing *The Redundant Male* by Jeremy Cherfas and John Gribbin, *Sunday Times,* 20th May, 1984

The male is a biological accident: the Y (male) chromosome is an incomplete X (female) chromosome, that is, has an incomplete set of genes. In other words, the male is an incomplete female, a walking abortion, aborted at the chromosome stage.

Valerie Solanas, *Scum Manifesto,* Matriarchy Study Group

Man is a complex being: he makes deserts bloom and lakes die.

Gil Stern, quoted in *Quotations for Our Time* (Dr. Laurence Peter)

PICKING ON MEN

Man seems to be a rickety sort of thing, any way you take him; a kind of British Museum of infirmities and inferiorities. He is always undergoing repairs. A machine that was as unreliable as he is would have no market.

Mark Twain, *Letters from the Earth*

What is a man? A miserable little pile of secrets.

André Malraux, quoted in *A Book of Quotes* (Barbara Rowes), Dutton

Men are monopolists
of 'stars, garters, buttons
and other shining baubles'—
unfit to be the guardians
of another person's happiness.

Marianne Moore, 'Marriage', *Collected Poems*

Man is an animal unfledged,
A monkey with his tail abridged;

His body flexible and limber,
And headed with a knob of timber;
A being frantic and unquiet,
And very fond of beer and riot.

His own best friend, and, you must know,
His own worst enemy by being so!

James Montgomery, 'Definition of Man',
quoted in *Stokes Cyclopaedia of Familiar Quotations* (Treffry)

man is a queer looking gink
who uses what brains he has
to get himself into trouble with
and then blames it on the fates.

Don Marquis, *Archy's Life of Mehitabel*

MEN, Definitions of

Men are those creatures with two legs and eight hands.

> **Jayne Mansfield,** quoted in *Dictionary of*
> *Contemporary Quotations* (Jonathon Green)

Men are no more than mischievous baboons.

> **Dr. William Harvey,** quoted in *Bartlett's*
> *Unfamiliar Quotations* (Leonard Louis Levinson)

Men are beasts and even beasts don't behave as they do.

> **Brigitte Bardot,** quoted in *A Book of*
> *Quotes* (Barbara Rowes), Dutton

Men are only animals anyway. They like to get out into the woods and growl round at night and feel something bite them.

> **Stephen Leacock,** *The Leacock*
> *Roundabout*, Dodd, Mead

Men are like flies—for men are insects too,
Little in mind, howe'er our bodies run!—
We're all insects: insects that hate each other,
And deem it love of God to hate one's brother.

> **Edward Irwin,** quoted in *The Nuttall*
> *Dictionary of Quotations* (James Wood)

Man is a military animal,
Glories in gunpowder and loves parade.

> **P.J. Bailey,** *Ibid*

At twenty a man is a peacock, at thirty a lion, at forty a camel, at fifty a serpent, at sixty a dog, at seventy an ape, at eighty nothing at all.

> **Baltasar Gracian,** *The Art of Worldly Wisdom*

When God made man, she was only testing.

> Graffito in ladies' lavatory, London W11

7

PICKING ON MEN

Me and my brother were talking to each other
About what makes a man a man.
Was it brains, was it brawn, or the month you were born.
We just couldn't understand.

Pete Townshend, 'Tattoo', Essex Music

Gentlemen

A gentleman is one who never hurts anyone's feelings unintentionally.

Oliver Herford, quoted in *Cassell's Book
of Humorous Quotations*

A gentleman is any man who wouldn't hit a woman with his hat on.

Fred Allen, quoted in *Peter's Quotations*
(Dr. Laurence Peter), Morrow

The criterion of a gentleman is that however poor he may be he still refuses to do useful work.

George Mikes, *How to be an Alien*

A gentleman is a patient wolf.

Henrietta Tiarks, quoted in *Handbook of
20th Century Quotations* (Frank S. Pepper)

A true gentleman is a man who knows how to play the bag-pipes—but doesn't.

Wall Street Journal, quoted in *Reader's
Digest,* March 1976

MEN

Physical Attributes of

Slugs and snails and puppy dogs tails.
That's what little boys are made of.

Traditional Nursery Rhyme

The beauty of stature is the only beauty of men.

Montaigne, 'Presumption', *Essays*

Woman has ovaries, a uterus . . . It is often said that she thinks
with her glands. Man superbly ignores the fact that his anatomy
also includes glands, such as the testicles, and that they secrete
hormones.

Simone de Beauvoir, *The Second Sex*

If women are supposed to be less rational and more emotional
at the beginning of our menstrual cycle when the female hor-
mone is at its lowest level, then why isn't it logical to say that,
in those few days, woman behave the most like the way men
behave all month long?

Gloria Steinem, *Outrageous Acts and*
Everyday Rebellions, 1984

PICKING ON MEN

What if female physicians decided that 'the monthly change in man's testosterone level so upsets his emotional equilibrium that he is unqualified for professional jobs' or that 'failure to accept the male role causes many of man's abdominal pains'?

Gena Corea, *The Hidden Malpractice*,
Morrow

So what would happen if suddenly, magically, men could menstruate and women could not? . . . Young boys would talk about it as the envied beginning of manhood. Gifts, religious ceremonies, family dinners and stag parties would mark the day . . .

Gloria Steinem, *Outrageous Acts and*
Everyday Rebellions

The Aranda (a tribe of Australian aborigines) . . . create in the male by the operation of sub-incision, a wound in the urethra which they call by their name for the female genital organ.

At certain ceremonials they make this 'Aralta-hole' bleed (to simulate a woman's menstrual period) but women are carefully excluded from these rites.

Ian D. Suttie, *The Origins of Love and Hate*,
Penguin

A man is two people, himself and his cock. A man always takes his friend to the party. Of the two, the friend is the nicer, being more able to show his feelings.

Beryl Bainbridge

The one statistic not given is the one Dr Kinsey also never gave. The insides and outsides of women are ransacked but no measurement is given for the penis.

Byron Rogers, reviewing 'Report of the
Task Group on Reference Men', *The*
Standard, 20th February, 1984

He (man) is proud that he has the biggest brain of all the primates, but attempts to conceal that he also has the biggest penis.

Desmond Morris, *The Naked Ape*

The penis is obviously going the way of the veriform appendix.

Jill Johnston, quoted in *Dictionary of Contemporary Quotations* (Jonathon Green)

Women do not feel about men's penises the way men seem to feel about women's vaginas.

Stephani Cook, *Second Life,* Michael Joseph

The daughter of a friend took her first bath with a male cousin when they were both four years old. Being well brought up, she was silent about her anatomical discovery, but that night, as her mother tucked her into bed, she said: 'Mommy, isn't it a blessing he doesn't have it on his face?'

So much for penis envy.

Carol Tavris, 'How Freud Betrayed Women', *Ms*, March 1984

It's no good looking for a joke
You've got one in your hand.

Graffito in gents' lavatory in Taunton, quoted in *Graffiti Lives OK* (Nigel Rees)

What is man, when you come to think upon him, but a minutely set, ingenious machine for turning, with infinite artfulness, the red wine of Shirez into urine.

Isak Dinesen, 'The Dreamers', *Seven Gothic Tales*

Never trust men with short legs. Brains too near their bottoms.

Noel Coward, quoted in *The Book of Insults* (Nancy McPhee)

PICKING ON MEN

Women have two X chromosomes; men an X and a Y, and the Y chromosome is only a deficient version of an X, 'A wretched-looking runt compared with the well-upholstered other chromosomes!' in Montagu's judgement, 'really a sad affair'. It was to their genetic deficiency 'that almost all the troubles to which the male falls heir may be traced, and to the presence of two well-appointed, well-furnished X chromosomes that the female owes her biological superiority.'

Barbara Ehrenreich, quoting Ashley Montagu in *The Hearts of Men*

It is the X and Y chromosomes which are responsible for determining the sex of the embryo. The ovum always contains an X chromosome but the sperm can vary between X and Y. If the sperm contains an X chromosome . . . the embryo will develop into a female. If it is a Y chromosome, it will develop into a male. Sometimes, despite the presence of the Y chromosome . . . the embryo develops into a female. (This implies that the basic human form is female.)

Patricia Welby, *A Book About Men* (Andrew Goodman and Patricia Welby)

→ *Adam's apple.* A protuberance in the throat of man, thoughtfully provided by nature to keep the rope in place.

Ambrose Bierce, *The Devil's Dictionary,* Penguin

MEN

Necessity for

In my opinion, to a woman who knows her own mind men can only be a minor consideration.

Maria Bashkirtseff, quoted in *The Wit of Women* (L. and M. Cowan)

I don't need them. I enjoy being alone.

Dyan Cannon, interviewed by Baz Bamigboye, *Daily Mail*, 1st September, 1984

A woman needs a man like a fish needs a bicycle.

Women's Liberation Slogan

If there are women who can help themselves, who go to work *and* run the home, then what are men for?

Diana Quick, quoted in *Woman Talk* (Michele Brown and Ann O'Connor)

There are only two kinds of men, the dead and the deadly.

Helen Rowland, quoted in *Handbook of 20th Century Quotations* (Frank S. Pepper)

. . . the male function is to produce sperm. We now have sperm banks.

Valerie Solanas, *Scum Manifesto,*
Matriarchy Study Group

Females could reproduce parthenogenetically if the egg cells could be induced to develop on their own. But males can never do so . . . Men are at best parasites on women, and at worst totally redundant in the immediate evolutionary scheme.

Jeremy Cherfas and John Gribbin, *The Redundant Male*

Sometimes I think if there was a third sex men wouldn't get so much as a glance from me.

Amanda Vail, *Love Me Little*

Men should only be the accessories of the strong woman.

Maria Bashkirtseff, quoted in *The Wit of Women* (L. and M. Cowan)

What vain, unnecessary things are men!
How well we do without 'em.

John Wilmot (Earl of Rochester),
quoted in *Oxford Dictionary of Quotations*

The male sex, as a sex, does not universally appeal to me. I find the men today less manly; but a woman of my age is not in a position to know exactly how manly they are.

Katharine Hepburn, quoted in *A Book of Quotes* (Barbara Rowes), Dutton

When I am dead you'll find it hard,
Said he,
To ever find another man
Like me.

What makes you think, as I suppose
You do,

14

I'd ever want another man
Like you?

Eugene Fitch Ware, in 'The Last Laugh',
Quoted in *Woman Talk* (Michele Brown and
Ann O'Connor)

A man said to the Universe;
'Sir, I exist!'
'However,' replied the Universe,
'The fact has not created in me
A sense of obligation.'

Stephen Crane, 'War is Kind', *Complete
Poems* (Joseph Katz), Cornell University
Press, 1972

MEN

Superiority of

There was, I think, never any reason to believe in any innate superiority of the male, except his superior muscle.

Bertrand Russell, *Unpopular Essays*

From the beginning, women recognized that male supremacy is baloney.

Marion Meade, *Bitching*

Male supremacy, like other political creeds, does not finally reside in physical strength but in acceptance of a value system which is not biological.

Kate Millett, quoted in *A Book of Quotes*
(Barbara Rowes), Dutton

Women rule the world . . . no man has ever done anything that a woman either hasn't allowed him to do or encouraged him to do.

Bob Dylan, *Rolling Stone,* 21st June, 1984

('Don't tell your father,' she had once said, 'but it's a fact that from the day they're born till the day they die, men are being protected by women.')

Anne Tyler, *The Clockwinder*

PICKING ON MEN

Men are by no means the more dominant, the more active, the more decisive half of the human race: why should they have to struggle so hard to pretend they are?

Andrew Goodman and Patricia Welby,
A Book About Men

Men's insistence on being of service sometimes expresses less consideration than girls like to believe. Helping women, treating them, bestowing gifts—these things are done much more for the donor's sake, as assertions of his superiority.

Dr. Rudolf Dreikurs, quoted in
Macmillan Treasury of Relevant Quotations
(Edward F. Murphy)

A man picks up a tramp because he wants a female companion who is no better than he is. In her company, he won't feel inferior. He rewards her by treating her like a lady.

Abigail Van Buren

I am a woman meant for a man, but I never found a man who could compete.

Bette Davis, quoted in *Woman Talk* (Michele
Brown and Ann O'Connor)

The boasted superiority of the men over our sex in the endowments of the mind is a mere commonplace vaunt.

Georgianna Anne Bellamy, quoted in
The Wit of Women (L. and M. Cowan)

Suffer women once to arrive at equality with you, and they will from that moment on become your superiors.

Cato the Elder

Failures are usually the most conceited of men.

D. H. Lawrence, quoted in *Quotations for
Our Time* (Dr. Laurence Peter)

When Lady Louise Moncrieff's last (16th) child was born her sister, Lady Elizabeth Arthur, was present and called out, 'It's all right, Louise, and you have got another little boy!' And the reply of the poor tired lady was: 'My dear, I really don't care if it's a parrot.'

> **Lord Ormathwaite,** quoted in *Handbook of 20th Century Quotations* (Frank S. Pepper)

Women have more imagination than men. They need it to tell us how wonderful we are.

> **Arnold H. Glasgow,** quoted in *Bartlett's Unfamiliar Quotations* (Leonard Louis Levinson)

The Government is making the dangerous assumption that the head of the household is always a man.

> **Gemma Hussey,** 'Sayings of the Week', *Observer*, 25th March, 1979

He was like a cock who thought the sun had risen to hear him crow.

> **George Eliot,** *Adam Bede*

Man was made when Nature was
But an apprentice, but women when she
Was a skilful mistress of her art.

> **Richard Crashaw,** quoted in *Encyclopaedia of Practical Quotations* (Hoyt), Funk & Wagnalls

The only really masterful noise a man ever makes in a house is the noise of his key, when he is still on the landing, fumbling for the lock.

> **Colette,** quoted in *The Wit of Women* (L. and M. Cowan)

PICKING ON MEN

In speech with a man a woman is at a disadvantage—because they speak different languages. She may understand his. Hers he will never speak or understand. In pity, or from some other motive, she must therefore, stammeringly, speak his. He listens and is flattered and thinks he has her mental measure when he has not touched even the fringe of her consciousness.

Dorothy Richardson, quoted in *Ms*,
March 1982

Real solemn history, I cannot be interested in . . . The quarrels of popes and kings, with wars or pestilences, in every page; the men all so good for nothing, and hardly any women at all.

Jane Austen, *Northanger Abbey*

Women on the whole tend to be nicer and more important, nearer to God than men.

Lord Arran, 'Sayings of the Week',
Observer, 20th July, 1975

Once made equal to man, woman becomes his superior.

Socrates, quoted in *Quotations for Our Time* (Dr. Laurence Peter)

MEN

Power Complex of

Poor little men! Poor little strutting peacocks! They spread out their tails as conquerors almost as soon as they are able to walk.

Jean Anouilh, *Cecile* (trans. Luce and Arthur Klein)

Male chauvinism . . . a shrewd method of extracting the maximum work for the minimum of compensation.

Michael Korda, *Male Chauvinism—How It Works*

The ultimate male chauvinism is to play the role of conquering hero and tyrant towards those greatest arch-women of all, Earth and Nature; to ignore their needs and break their rules, to use, exploit and subdue them with the rapist's violence and lack of love.

Beata Bishop with Pat McNeill, *Below the Belt*

The male sex still constitutes in many ways the most obstinate vested interest one can find.

Lord Longford, quoted in *Penguin Dictionary of Modern Quotations* (J.M. and M.J. Cohen)

. . . men look to destroy every quality in a woman which will give her the powers of a male, for she is in their eyes already armed with the power that brought them forth . . .

Norman Mailer, interviewed by Kate Millett, quoted in *Man's World, Woman's Place* (Elizabeth Janeway), Dell

They've equated their sex with power for so long that now they're faced with losing power they scream about being emasculated.

Anon, quoted by Jill Tweedie, *Guardian,* 2nd February, 1970

If any man had proved sufficiently self-centred and commonplace to attempt my subjugation, I should have judged him, found him wanting and left him. The only sort of person in whose favour I could ever wish to surrender my autonomy would be just the one who did his utmost to prevent any such thing.

Simone de Beauvoir, *Observer,* 1974

Boys bring in to the school the values and experiences of a woman-hating culture, and most of them intend to teach the women and girls they encounter there the many lessons of male supremacy—lessons which the male teachers either endorse or do nothing to counter.

Anon, 'Sexual Harassment in Schools' *Spare Rib,* June 1982

Men control the political scene—internationally as well as nationally. They make the wars and make the treaties. They control international finance. They make and interpret most of the laws, many of them disadvantageous to women, poor people, blacks, American Indians, Puerto Ricans, etc. While there are outstanding exceptions in the case of individuals, the male domination in many areas has been singularly insensitive to the needs of the weak.

Coretta Scott King, quoted in *Macmillan Treasury of Relevant Quotations* (Edward F. Murphy)

Congress is a middle-aged, middle-class, white male power structure . . . no wonder it's been so totally unresponsive to the needs of this country.

Bella Abzug, quoted by Gloria Steinem in
Outrageous Acts and Everyday Rebellions

. . . every little white Christian boy in the class thinks he is the one who is supposed to be the President. That is why little white Christian boys often seem so much less interesting than little black or Jewish or Chicano or Chinese boys, or than any sort of little girl: little white Christian boys are under a lot of White House pressure.

Calvin Trillin, *Uncivil Liberties*

Only one man in a thousand is a leader of men - the other 999 follow women.

Groucho Marx, quoted in *Handbook of
20th Century Quotations* (Frank S. Pepper)

I got no more respect for the big man. Pulling me down to what he understands. He can't get his mind around no bigger plans.

Nancy and Ann Wilson, song lyric, Epic
Records

The true micro-junkie is almost always male. 'I think that's because men are more leery of emotion and keener on establishing control,' says Dr. Antonia Jones, a researcher into artificial intelligence at Brunel University.

Dr. Antonia Jones, interviewed by Jane
Firbank, *Mail on Sunday*, 21st October, 1984

In 'A Woman's Place' (BBC1) the executive producer was a man, the producer was a man, the cameramen were men, the film editor was a man, the dubbing mixer was a man, the commentary was spoken by a man . . . Oh, God, who is also a man, it makes me tired.

Nancy Banks-Smith, TV review,
Guardian, 28th January, 1970

Status symbols are a masculine thing, aren't they?

Christina Foyle, 'Sayings of the Week',
Observer, 16th October, 1977

The crass ingratitude of haughty man,
Vested in all the pride of place and power,
Brooks not the aspirations of my sex,
However just.

Sarah Anne Curzon (1887), quoted in
*Dictionary of Canadian Quotations and
Phrases* (Robert M. Hamilton and Dorothy Shields)

I react against the plain, the one-dimensional men . . . I meet them everywhere, prosaic, down-to-earth, always talking of politics, never for one moment in the world of music or pleasure, never free of the weight of daily problems, never joyous, never elated, made of either concrete and steel or like work horses, indifferent to their bodies, obsessed with power.

Anaïs Nin, *The Diaries of Anaïs Nin*

The men who really wield, retain and covet power are the kind who answer bedside telephones while making love.

Nicholas Pileggi, quoted in *A Book of
Quotes* (Barbara Rowes), Dutton

Man, proud man,
Dressed in a little brief authority,
Most ignorant of what he's most assured,
His glossy essence, like an angry ape,

24

Plays such fantastic tricks before high heaven
As make the angels weep.

William Shakespeare, *Measure for Measure*

All Men would be tyrants if they could . . . That your Sex are Naturally Tyrannical is a Truth so thoroughly established as to admit of no dispute.

Abigail Adams, to John Adams (March 1776), quoted in *Ms*, July 1975

MEN

Macho Image of

Macho does not prove mucho.

Zsa Zsa Gabor

When two men fight over a woman, it's the fight they want not the woman.

Brendan Francis, quoted in *Macmillan Treasury of Relevant Quotations* (Edward F. Murphy)

Many men are a good deal more interested in proving their masculinity to other men than they are in the woman herself.

Jill Tweedie, *Guardian,* 6th April, 1970

If, as men, we think of sex as a competitive sport or a mechanical exercise, it is because we are afraid to face it for what it is. We like to control the situation because we are afraid of what would happen if we didn't. Behind the 'masculine' stud talk and the obsessions with maintaining erections, lies nothing less than a terror of what would happen if we lost control.

Andrew Goodman, *A Book About Men* (Andrew Goodman and Patricia Welby)

PICKING ON MEN

The male stereotype makes masculinity not just a fact of biology but something that must be proved and re-proved, a continual quest for an ever-receding Holy Grail.

Marc Feigen Fasteau, *The Male Machine*,
McGraw-Hill

In the past, it was easy to be a Real Man. All you had to do was abuse women, steal land from Indians, and find someplace to dump the toxic waste.

Bruce Feirstein, *Real Men Don't Eat Quiche*, 1982

. . . almost universally a man can divorce a wife who is barren . . . This holds despite the fact that it may be the husband who is at fault. Men do not accept male infertility.

Jeremy Cherfas and John Gribbin, *The Redundant Male*

The bitterest creature under heaven is the wife who discovers that her husband's bravery is only bravado, that his strength is only a uniform, that his power is but a gun in the hands of a fool.

Pearl S. Buck, *To My Daughters With Love*

We wouldn't have a male-dominated world today if men hadn't an eternity ago denied and banished their feminine nature into some deep and forgotten layer of their selves. If you as much as mention the subject to a so-called average man, he'll promptly think that you are doubting his 100 per cent virility and react with manly anger.

Beata Bishop with Pat McNeill, *Below The Belt*

The extent of their success (the Greenham women) in using woman power on behalf of a key woman's objective—peace— is to be found in the anger they arouse in the macho male.

Barbara Castle, *Guardian*, 2nd October, 1984

Men make a cult of everything that's aggressively masculine, and ridicule its opposite. They are proud of not being able to understand women, thereby implying that women with their so-called irrational thinking and unpredictable emotions cannot be understood by any sane being.

Beata Bishop with Pat McNeill, *Below the Belt*

The young macho male either models himself on a rock star . . . he'll grandly grant you the right to do what you like—as long as it doesn't interfere with his dinner. Alternatively he simply fails to understand what all the fuss is about, and continues to treat you like a cross between his nanny and an inflatable doll . . . Don't worry . . . these groups can be largely ignored.

Cathy Douglas, *The Superwoman Trap*

Whether, as some psychologists believe, women suffer from penis envy, I am not sure. I am quite certain, however, that all males without exception suffer from penis rivalry, and that this trait has now become a threat to the future existence of the human race.

W. H. Auden, *A Certain World*

Since it is men, not women, who suffer from penis envy, Freud seems to have viewed the problem backwards.

Marion Meade, *Bitching*

Freud, of course, was wrong when he claimed that women suffer from penis envy—it is the men who do.

Sabina Sedgewick, *Ladies' Home Erotica,*
Ten Speed Press, 1981

We'll have a swashing and a martial outside,
As many other mannish cowards have
That do outface it with their semblance.

William Shakespeare, *As You Like It*

PICKING ON MEN

Men's lives are dominated by vanity and competition, they always play at cowboys or sheriff.

François Truffaut, 'Take One'

John Wayne is supposed to be masculinity personified but to me he represents stupidity, rigidity and boredom—the masculine thing is very boring.

Rene Daalder, quoted by Jill Tweedie,
Guardian, 2nd February, 1970

The tragedy of machismo is that a man is never quite man enough.

Germaine Greer, 'My Mailer Problem',
1971

What have Hemingway and Hefner and Bogart and (even) John Kennedy and Charles Atlas and the sins of our fathers before them done to our males that they continue to labour under their own ghostly machismo?—which must be the loneliest, most fragile state in the world, this worship of form without content.

Cynthia Buchanan, *New York Times,* 9th
February, 1972

It is unrelievedly everything. It is long, loud, male and nihilistic, and you can put those in any order of importance, because they are all responsible for one another.

Russell Davies, reviewing *Cross of Iron,*
Observer, 13th February, 1977

I've never found brawn appealing. If I went out with Macho Man I think I'd have a permanent headache. Kind of 'You Tarzan— Mi-graine.'

Overheard on a bus

Of course men are dreadfully hung up on their virility, so they drive big cars, drink vodka and make rude cracks to undermine each other's sex life.

Anon journalist, quoted by Carol Dix in 'Who's Afraid of the Female Sex Drive', *Cosmopolitan*, May 1974

A Good Ole Boy is not simply a man who makes a to-do out of his masculinity—most men do a little of that. He makes such an incessant fetish out of it that he becomes gamey, or pathetic, or both.

Florence King, *Southern Ladies and Gentlemen*, Stein & Day

My advice to any girl anxious to explore the world outside her home after marriage, is to choose a man not only intelligent and capable, but above all one who is able to cook a light meal without regarding it as a slur on his virility.

The Rt Hon. Baroness Summerskill, quoted in *The Wit of Women* (L. and M. Cowan)

Men who are insecure about their masculinity often challenge me to fights.

Honor Blackman, quoted in *Woman Talk* (Michele Brown and Ann O'Connor)

Men's men: gentle or simple, they're much of a muchness.

George Eliot, *Daniel Deronda*

Men, with all their bravado, seldom have the courage to stick a flower on their desks.

Alan Alda

MEN

Violence of

Today a doctor could make a million dollars if he could figure a way to bring a boy into the world without a trigger finger.

Arthur Miller, quoted in *A Book of Quotes*
(Barbara Rowes), Dutton

Dozens of studies show that males of all ages engage in more physical aggression, fantasy aggression, verbal aggression and play aggression than females do.

Eleanor Maccoby and Carol Jacklin,
quoted by Philip Hodson, *Observer*, 10th
February, 1980

Every normal man must be tempted at times to spit on his hands, hoist the black flag, and begin slitting throats.

H. L. Mencken, quoted in *Macmillan
Treasury of Relevant Quotations* (Edward F.
Murphy)

Man, biologically considered . . . is the most formidable of all the beasts of prey, and, indeed, the only one that preys systematically on its own species.

William James

PICKING ON MEN

Men! The only animal in the world to fear.

D. H. Lawrence, Mountain Lion

Man is the only animal to whom the torture and death of his fellow creatures is amusing in itself.

James A. Froude, quoted in Peter's
Quotations (Dr. Laurence Peter), Morrow

A man out of temper does not wait for proofs before feeling toward all things, animate and inanimate, as if they were in a conspiracy against him, but at once thrashes his horse or kicks his dog in consequence.

George Eliot, The Mill on the Floss

There can be no double standard. We cannot have peace among men whose hearts find delight in killing any living creature.

Rachel Carson, quoted in Woman Talk
(Michele Brown and Ann O'Connor)

It's as if some men were saying: 'You won't stay weak enough for me to hold the door open for you? Okay, I'll slam it on your hand.'

Florynce Kennedy, quoted by Gloria
Steinem, Ms, April 1980

Men are less afraid of injuring one who awakens love than one who inspires fear.

Machiavelli, quoted in The Nuttall
Dictionary of Quotations (James Wood)

Lavender is grown for its fragrant flowers . . . The Kaybyle women of North Africa think it protects them from maltreatment by their husbands. Most American women know better.

Katherine White, Onward and Upward in
the Garden, 1979

Male sexual aggression seemed to be taken for granted by students of both sexes. 'What do you expect—a lot of guys are animals', one man comments amiably. 'Well, you always try to score—how far you push it depends on who you are', says his room-mate. 'Or how drunk you are', a third chimes in.

Karen Barrett, 'Date Rape', *Ms*,
September 1982

The result of the latest study, discussed at a symposium on the effects of violence pornography at the Meeting of the American Psychological Association, showed that nearly a third of the men watching films portraying extreme violence against women (even where not explicit) were stimulated and more likely to accept rapists' attitudes.

Jeannette Kupfermann, 'Victims of a
New Guilt', *Sunday Times*, 9th
September, 1984

There are an awful lot of loony men in London. Every woman you know has a tale to tell—of actual assault, of the threat, or just of the kind of male behaviour that leads you to go about more warily than before. What kind of liberation can there be under curfew?

Valerie Grove, *The Standard*, 12th
October, 1984

. . . when I say that London is full of loony men it is no jest or game, because these men are vicious and menacing and however pathetic or screwed up or lonely they are inside their heads, we are unmoved because they circumscribe our lives and hinder our freedom.

Valerie Grove, *Ibid*

Mad or sane, it's men who are violent and women who are victims.

Jill Tweedie, quoted by Paul Kerton, *Over 21*, March 1984

All men are rapists and that's all they are. They rape us with their eyes, their laws and their cocks.

Marilyn French, quoted in *Dictionary of Contemporary Quotations* (Jonathon Green)

Sexual aggression and insult is not abnormal, isolated behaviour; it is inherent in the conversational mythology of contempt, cynical sensuality and unpleasant laughter in which most men are happy to participate . . . Women must certainly not allow themselves to be misled by the snivelling and bluster which is the normal masculine response when the issue of this sort of sexual intimidation is raised.

Godfrey Marriott, letter to *The Standard*, 9th November, 1984

Talk to any group of five or six women. One of them was probably sexually abused as a child by a man in her own family circle.

Florynce Kennedy, quoted in *Outrageous Acts and Everyday Rebellions* (Gloria Steinem)

From prehistoric times to the present, I believe, rape has played a critical function. It is nothing more or less than a conscious process of intimidation by which all men keep all women in a state of fear.

Susan Brownmiller, *Against Our Will*, Simon & Schuster

We're continually the victims of violence; we're mugged, we're raped, we're beaten and not by women. It's not ridicule I fear from men, it's physical violence.

Anon, quoted by Jill Tweedie, *Guardian*, 2nd February, 1970

Women get beaten, raped, murdered and mutilated only by men. Men do not fear this from women.

Glenda Gerrard, letter in the *Guardian*,
23rd October, 1984

Men believe that it is acceptable to hit women; a belief that is only shaken when the woman leaves.

Anon, 'News', *Spare Rib*, April 1982

Even nice, reasonable men seem to believe that a woman who enjoys sex has a secret wish to be raped. But nice, reasonable women don't believe that a man who enjoys a drink has a secret wish to have a stranger force a jugful of dirty water down his throat.

Anon

Last month a father was convicted of raping his six daughters as they grew up, one by one. This man was sentenced to FOUR years in prison, and a newspaper wanted to know 'Where was the mother? Why didn't she put a stop to it?' In the same period, two mothers have been convicted of murdering the husband of one of them, who had been raping both their daughters. These women have been sentenced to TWENTY-FOUR years in prison.

J. Meyer (Venice), letter to *Spare Rib*, April 1984

The flashers, grabbers, bottom-pinchers, purse snatchers, kerb-crawlers, verbal abusers, peeping Toms and the ultimate cowards, the ones who roam in packs, have left an indelible impression on women's minds and—more in anger than in fear—women are determined to evade, forestall and undermine these invaders of our freedom.

Valerie Grove, *The Standard*, 5th
November, 1984

PICKING ON MEN

That gentlemen prefer blondes is due to the fact that, apparently, pale hair, delicate skin and an infantile expression represent the very apex of a frailty which every man longs to violate.

Alexander King, quoted in *Cassell's Book of Humorous Quotations*

No one assumed that because men had castration anxieties—i.e. fantasies—they wanted to be castrated.

Molly Haskell, 'Rape Fantasy', *Ms,* November 1976

Older men send younger men to fight, white men send men of colour, rich men send poor men. In war, perhaps as in no other situation, many men experience life as women live it—subject to the dictates of others, and threatened by a violence not of their creation.

Julie Melrose, *Ms,* October 1980

Men love war because it allows them to look serious. Because it is the one thing that stops women laughing at them.

John Fowles, *The Magus*

If girls fired guns and women generals planned the battles, then the men would feel there was no morality to war—they would have no one to fight for, nowhere to leave their consciences. War would appear to them as savage and pointless as it really is. The men want the women to stay out of the fighting so they can give it meaning.

Ian McEwan, 'The Imitation Game', BBC1, 24th April, 1980

I am fed up with a system which busts the pot smoker and lets the big dope racketeers go free. I am sick of old men dreaming up wars for young men to die in.

George McGovern, 'Sayings of the
Week', *Observer,* 9th April, 1972

All wars are planned by old men in council rooms apart.

Grantland Rice, 'Two Sides of War'

Old men declare war. But it is the youth that must fight and die.

Herbert C. Hoover, quoted in *Handbook of
20th Century Quotations* (Frank S. Pepper)

Military men are the scourges of the world.

Guy de Maupassant, quoted in
Quotations for Our Time (Dr. Laurence
Peter)

Because men are too emotional to vote. Their conduct at baseball games and political conventions shows this, while their innate tendency to appeal to force renders them particularly unfit for the task of government.

Anon, 'Why Men Shouldn't Have The Vote'
(letter to the Editor), *Ms,* 1973

A man may build himself a throne of bayonets, but he cannot sit on it.

Dean Inge, *Wit and Wisdom of Dean Inge*

MEN

Fears Suffered by

One reason women's liberation petrifies men is that, for the first time in their lives, they are hearing women say *publicly* exactly the things they've been revealing to each other *privately* for centuries.

Marion Meade, *Bitching*

It takes a brave man to face a brave woman, and man's fear of women's creative energy has never found expression more clear than in the old German clamor, renewed by the Nazis, of 'Kinder, Kuchen und Kirche' for women.

Pearl S. Buck, *To My Daughters with Love*

My literary reputation—or rather the lack of it—is the work of male reviewers who fear female sexuality and don't like successful women.

Erica Jong, interviewed by Anthea
Disney, *Observer*, 12th October, 1980

Behind men's often petty attitude toward successful women lies the fear of women's acquiring power, both the power to live their own lives independently and the power to influence the lives of men.

Michael Korda, *Male Chauvinism—How It Works*

Indeed, I should say without reservation that men fear and hate women more than women fear and hate men. I think it is this rather than the male's superior strength that makes it possible for our civilization to be called 'a man's world'. It is not a contest of strength; it is a contest of hate.

Dr. Karl Menninger, *A Psychiatrist's World*, Viking Press.

Men are nervous of remarkable women.

J. M. Barrie, *What Every Woman Knows*, 1908

If a person continues to see only giants, it means he is still looking at the world through the eyes of a child. I have a feeling that man's fear of women comes from having first seen her as the mother, creator of men.

Anaïs Nin, *Diary*, Harcourt, Brace & World

Beauty, like male ballet dancers, makes some men afraid.

Mordecai Richler, quoted in *Canadian Dictionary of Quotations and Phrases* (Robert M. Hamilton and Dorothy Shields)

Men don't know how to deal with fear. Women deal with birth and death all their lives and are less frightened to face it. When a man says that a woman is emotional, it usually means that he is emotional but covering it up with his intellect.

Dora Russell, talking to Pat Kitto, *Spare Rib*, July 1982

A man will try anything with a woman, but he won't vote for her.

Dale Messich, *Ms*, December 1975

I remember one political colleague (a man, of course) saying to me all those years ago: 'Of course, I think you should be in Parliament, but unfortunately women won't vote for a woman.' The typical alibi of the threatened male.

Barbara Castle, *Guardian,* 2nd October, 1984

There is no question that men have a great deal of hostility toward women.

Mario Puzo, 'Confessions of a Male Chauvinist', *Cosmopolitan,* December 1972

Probably the only place where a man can feel really secure is in a maximum security prison.

Germaine Greer

MEN

Wisdom and Intelligence of

The average man's opinions are much less foolish than they would be if he thought for himself.

> Attributed to **Bertrand Russell,** quoted
> in *Penguin Dictionary of Modern Quotations*
> (J.M. and M.J. Cohen)

It is impossible to defeat an ignorant man in argument.

> **William G. McAdoo,** quoted in *The
> Public Speaker's Treasure Chest* (Herbert
> V. Prochnow and Herbert V. Prochnow Jr.)

As a rule, a man who doesn't know his own mind hasn't missed much.

> **Herbert V. Prochnow and Herbert V.
> Prochnow Jr.,** *Ibid.*

A fellow who's always declaring he's no fool usually has his suspicions.

> **Wilson Mizner,** quoted in *Bartlett's
> Unfamiliar Quotations* (Leonard Louis Levinson)

Men are mostly so slow, their thoughts over-run 'em an' they can only catch 'em by the tail.

> **George Eliot**

Men occasionally stumble over the truth, but most of them pick themselves up and hurry off as if nothing had happened.

> **Winston Churchill,** quoted in *Treasury of Humorous Quotations* (Esar)

Men deride what they do not understand, and snarl at the good and beautiful because it lies beyond their sympathies.

> **Goethe,** quoted in *The Nuttall Dictionary of Quotations* (James Wood)

A man's mind, what there is of it—has always the advantage of being masculine,—as the smallest birch tree is of a higher kind than the most soaring palm,—and even his ignorance is of a sounder quality.

> **George Eliot,** *Middlemarch*

At the bottom of the modern man there is always a great thirst for self-forgetfulness, self-distraction . . . and therefore he turns away from all those problems and abysses which might recall to him his own nothingness.

> **Henri Frederic Amiel,** quoted in *Quotations for Our Time* (Dr. Laurence Peter)

Man does not want to know. When he knows very little he plays with the possibilities of knowledge, but when he finds that the pieces he has been putting together are going to spell out the answer he is frightened and he throws them in every direction; and another civilization falls.

> **Dame Rebecca West,** quoted in *Rebecca West: Artist and Thinker* (Peter Wolfe), Southern Illinois University Press, 1971

The trouble about man is twofold. He cannot learn truths which are too complicated; he forgets truths which are too simple.

> **Dame Rebecca West,** quoted in *The Wit of Women* (L. and M. Cowan)

Men can see through a barn door, they can. Perhaps that's the reason they can see so little o' this side on't.

George Eliot, *Adam Bede*

There are men who would even be afraid to commit themselves on the doctrine that castor oil is a laxative.

Cammille Flammarion, quoted in
Bartlett's Unfamiliar Quotations (Leonard Louis Levinson)

Germany will either be a world power or will not be.

Adolf Hitler, *Mein Kampf,* quoted in
Handbook of 20th Century Quotations
(Frank S. Pepper)

I never could find a man who could think for two minutes together.

Sydney Smith, *Sketches of Moral Philosophy*

It is a sorry business to inquire into what men think, when we are every day only too uncomfortably confronted with what they do.

Michael Arlen, *The Three-Cornered Moon,*
quoted in *Penguin Dictionary of Modern
Quotations* (J.M. and M.J. Cohen)

Oh, what men dare do! What men may do! What men daily do, not knowing what they do!

William Shakespeare, *Much Ado About Nothing*

Men are most apt to believe what they least understand.

Pliny, quoted in *The Nuttall Dictionary of
Quotations* (James Wood)

Men are always ready to respect anything that bores them.

Marilyn Monroe, quoted in *A Book of
Quotes* (Barbara Rowes), Dutton

PICKING ON MEN

Young men think old men fools, and old men know young men to be so.

Quoted by Camden as a saying of one
Dr. Victor Howard Metcalf, in *Stokes
Cyclopaedia of Familiar Quotations*
(Treffry)

In the country of the blind a one-eyed King can still goof it up.

Dr. Laurence Peter, *Quotations for Our Time*

All the reasoning of men is not worth one sentiment of women.

Voltaire, *Maxims*

The bitter truth about women is that their minds work precisely like those of men; the bitter truth about men is they are too vain to admit it.

Robertson Davies, *Samuel Marchbanke's Almanac*

Men are more conventional then women and much slower to change their ideas.

Kathleen Norris, quoted in *Macmillan
Treasury of Relevant Quotations* (Edward F.
Murphy)

A woman need know but one man well, in order to understand all men; whereas a man may know all women and understand not one of them.

Helen Rowland, quoted in *The Wit of
Women* (L. and M. Cowan)

However dull a woman may be, she will understand all there is of life; however intelligent a man may be, he will never know half of it.

Madame Fée, *Ibid.*

Ask a woman for a description of a person and you will get the lot from height and colouring to if they have good teeth and plucked eyebrows. Ask a man and you will probably get 'Well, average really'

Zena Scott Archer, interviewed by
Angela Levin, *Observer*, 6th November, 1977

Throughout history, females have picked providers for mates. Males pick anything.

Margaret Mead, quoted in *Woman Talk*
(Michele Brown and Ann O'Connor)

The reason the all-American boy prefers beauty to brains is that the all-American boy can see better than he can think.

Farrah Fawcett Majors

God made men stronger but not necessarily more intelligent. He gave women intuition and femininity. And, used properly, that combination easily jumbles the brain of any man I've ever met.

Farrah Fawcett Majors, quoted in *A Book of Quotes* (Barbara Rowes), Dutton

Men do not make their homes unhappy because they have genius, but because they have not enough genius.

William Wordsworth, quoted in *The Nuttall Dictionary of Quotations* (James Wood)

Clever men are mostly such unpleasant animals.

D. H. Lawrence, quoted in *Penguin Dictionary of Modern Quotations* (J.M. and M.J. Cohen)

All down the ages, the stupid men have been swatting the clever men on the jaw. It's their only retort.

Fred Jacob, quoted in *Dictionary of Canadian Quotations and Phrases* (Robert M. Hamilton and Dorothy Shields)

PICKING ON MEN

Men are led by trifles.

Napoleon, quoted in *The Nuttall Dictionary of Quotations* (James Wood)

Men . . . have no perceptive power, no intuition and no control. How can we help acting stupid?

Anon male, quoted in *Sex Tips for Girls* (Cynthia Heimel)

In his private heart, no man much respects himself.

Mark Twain, quoted in *Quotations for Our Time* (Dr. Laurence Peter)

The young man who has not wept is a savage, and the old man who will not laugh is a fool.

George Santayana, quoted in *Penguin Dictionary of Modern Quotations* (J.M. and M.J. Cohen)

They are so obsessed by public affairs that they see the world as by moonlight, which shows the outlines of every object but not the details indicative of their nature.

Rebecca West, quoted in *Macmillan Treasury of Relevant Quotations* (Edward F. Murphy)

There are more fools than wise men and even in the wise man himself there is more folly than wisdom.

Nicholas Chamfort, quoted in *Treasury of Humorous Quotations* (Esar)

MEN

Romantic Idealism of

Some men can live up to their loftiest ideals without ever going higher than the basement.

Austin O'Malley, quoted in *Treasury of Humorous Quotations* (Esar)

The average man takes all the natural taste out of his food by covering it with ready-made sauces, and all the personality out of a woman by covering her with his ready-made ideals.

Helen Rowland, *A Guide to Men,* Dodge Publishing Co., 1922

Every man wants a woman to appeal to his better side, his nobler instincts and his higher nature—and another woman to make him forget them.

Helen Rowland, *Ibid.*

Men love putting women on a pedestal because it's so much more satisfying when they knock them off. They fall farther.

Clare Boothe Luce

Nothing spoils a romance so much as a sense of humour in the woman.

Oscar Wilde

PICKING ON MEN

Men are still desperately looking for the small concessions that will allow them to preserve their greater illusions, unable to face a life that has to be lived, ultimately, among equals, in which the possession of a penis does not serve as a substitute for brains, charm or originality, in which no status attaches to it by divine right.

Michael Korda, *Male Chauvinism—How It Works*

Men may be allowed romanticism; women, who can create life in their own bodies, dare not indulge in it.

Phyllis McGinley, quoted in *Woman Talk* (Michele Brown and Ann O'Connor)

The making of Utopias is a masculine foible. I cannot recall any Utopia written by a woman; though most of them contain laws which women would resist either by the ancient method of a strike, as described by Aristophanes in The Lysistrata, or by the modern method of bombs. Most Utopias have been written by Englishmen or Frenchmen.

Dean Inge, *Lay Thoughts*

Men run away to other countries because they are not good in their own, and run back to their own because they pass for nothing in the new places.

Ralph Waldo Emerson, quoted in *The Nuttall Dictionary of Quotations* (James Wood)

Men are all the same. They always think that something they are going to get is better than what they have got.

John Oliver Hobbes, quoted in *Macmillan Treasury of Relevant Quotations* (Edward F. Murphy)

Wives invariably flourish when deserted; it is the deserting male, the reckless idealist rushing about the world seeking a non-existent felicity, who often ends in disaster.

William McFee, quoted in *Woman Talk*
(Michele Brown and Ann O'Connor)

A woman can forgive a man the harm he does her; but she can never forgive him for the sacrifices he makes on her account.

Somerset Maugham, *The Moon and
Sixpence*

Why, as Lady Haberton put it, should it be supposed 'that the male form came perfect from the hands of the Creator, while that of the female needs constant tinkering and screwing into shape to make it presentable'?

Lisa Tickner, *Spare Rib,* October 1976

Every man has a sane spot somewhere.

Robert Louis Stevenson, quoted in
Barlett's Unfamiliar Quotations (Leonard
Louis Levinson)

Whenever a man exclaims that all mankind are villains, be assured that he contemplates an instant offer of himself as an exception.

Douglas Jerrold, quoted in *Treasury of
Humorous Quotations* (Esar)

Young men want to be faithful and are not;
Old men want to be faithless and are not.

Oscar Wilde, *The Picture of Dorian Grey*

PICKING ON MEN

If biologists are right in their assertion that there is not a perfect man today on the face of the globe, a lot of personal opinions here and there will have to be altered.

Quoted in *The Public Speaker's Treasure Chest* (Herbert V. Prochnow and Herbert V. Prochnow Jr.), A. Thomas of Preston

MEN

Spiritual Aspirations of

I never wonder to see men wicked, but I often wonder to see them not ashamed.

Jonathan Swift, *Thoughts on Various Subjects*

Men like advising the women better than doing right themselves.

C. H. Spurgeon, quoted in *The Nuttall Dictionary of Quotations* (James Wood)

I never knew any man in my life who could not bear another's misfortunes perfectly like a Christian.

Alexander Pope, quoted in *International Thesaurus of Quotations* (Rhoda Thomas Tripp), Penguin

A Christian is a man who feels repentance on a Sunday for what he did on Saturday and is going to do on Monday.

Thomas R. Ybarra, quoted in *Quotations for Our Time* (Dr. Laurence Peter)

If men were angels, no government would be necessary.

James Madison, quoted in *Quotations in History* (Alan and Veronica Palmer)

PICKING ON MEN

If man is only a little lower than the angels, the angels should reform.

Mary Wilson Little, quoted in *Handbook of 20th Century Quotations* (Frank S. Pepper)

Poor, dismal, ugly, sterile, shabby little man . . . with your scrabble of harsh oaths—Joy, glory and magnificence were here for you . . . but you scrabbled along . . . rattling a few stale words . . . and would have none of them.

Thomas Clayton Wolfe, quoted in *Quotations for Our Time* (Dr. Laurence Peter)

As a man is so's his God; this word
Explains why God's so often absurd.

Giles and Melville Harcourt, *Short Prayers for the Long Day*

It's a curious fact that the all-male religions have produced no religious imagery—in most cases have positively forbidden it. The great religious art of the world is deeply involved with the female principle.

Kenneth (Lord) Clark, *Civilisation*

Abasement: an act of faith when a man decides he is not God.

Oliver Wendell Holmes, *The Wit's Dictionary* (Colin Bowles)

MEN

And Women

If I were a girl I'd despair. The supply of good women far exceeds that of the men who'd deserve them.

> **Robert Graves,** 'Woman's Day', *Collected Poems*, Cassell

Men continually study women, and know nothing about them. Women never study men, and know all about them.

> **Robert C. Edwards,** quoted in *Dictionary of Canadian Quotations and Phrases* (Robert M. Hamilton and Dorothy Shields)

Women know men better than they know themselves and better than men ever suspect.

> **Sir John Willison,** *Personal and Political Reminiscences*

Women know women. And Women know that Women know men. And Women know that men do not know Women.

> **Arnold Haultain,** *Hints for Lovers*, Constable, 1910

PICKING ON MEN

Several men I can think of are as capable, as smart, as funny, as compassionate, and as confused—as remarkable you might say—as most women.

Jane Howard

A woman's guess is much more accurate than a man's certainty.

Rudyard Kipling, *Plain Tales from the Hills*

Women's rougher, simpler, more upright judgement embraces the whole truth, which their tact, and their mistrust of masculine idealism, ever prevents them from speaking in its entirety.

Joseph Conrad, *Chance,* quoted in *Who Said That?* (Renie Gee)

. . . behind every mediocre man, there is usually a woman who has given her life to establish his.

Andrew Goodman, *A Book About Men* (Andrew Goodman and Patricia Welby)

Behind every successful man stands a surprised woman.

Maryon Pearson, quoted in *Dictionary of Canadian Quotations and Phrases* (Robert M. Hamilton and Dorothy Shields)

Behind almost every woman you ever heard of stands a man who let her down.

Naomi Bliven, quoted in *The Wit of Women* (L. and M. Cowan)

There's a great women behind every idiot.

John Lennon

Women want mediocre men, and men are working hard to be as mediocre as possible.

Margaret Mead, quoted in *Handbook of 20th Century Quotations* (Frank S. Pepper)

MEN, And Women

I'm not denyin' the women are foolish;
God Almighty made 'em to match the men.

George Eliot, *Adam Bede*

The male is docile and easily led, easily subjected to the domination of any female who cares to dominate him.

Valerie Solanas, *Scum Manifesto,* Matriarchy Study Group

No man is a match for a woman, except with a poker and a pair of hobnailed boots. Not always even then.

George Bernard Shaw, *Man and Superman*

Men are rarely intrepid in the presence of women; but women rarely stand in awe of men.

Arnold Haultain, quoted in *Dictionary of Canadian Quotations and Phrases* (Robert M. Hamilton and Dorothy Shields)

No one can make a man look a fool quite so successfully as a woman. Any man: any woman.

Ray Connolly, *The Standard,* 15th October, 1984

I cannot remember a single masculine figure created by a woman who is not, at bottom, a booby.

H.L. Mencken, quoted in *Penguin Dictionary of Modern Quotations* (J.M. and M.J. Cohen)

A woman would no doubt need a great deal of imagination to love a man for his virtue.

John Oliver Hobbes, *The Sinner's Comedy*

No woman ever falls in love with a man unless she has a better opinion of him than he deserves.

Ed Howe, quoted in *Quotations for Our Time* (Dr. Laurence Peter)

PICKING ON MEN

You have to wrap everything up in cotton wool when you are dealing with a man, and flatter him up to the eyebrows. You can deal directly and honestly with a woman.

Winifred Ewing, MP, quoted in *The Wit of Women*
(L. and M. Cowan)

Women have served all these centuries as looking glasses possessing the magic and delicious power of reflecting the figure of a man at twice its natural size.

Virginia Woolf, *A Room of One's Own*

Men have taken the easy way out, making half the species their audience, looking out toward it for an applause which is becoming fainter and fainter, putting on a show that is already dusty with age, made up of tired jokes and creaking routines, an ancient hit which deserves to die a merciful death. The time has come to pack up the scenery.

Michael Korda, *Male Chauvinism—How It Works*

Women live both sensually and intellectually. Men are amateurs, women are professionals.

François Truffaut, 'Take One'

Women are the only oppressed group in our society that lives in intimate association with our oppressors.

Evelyn Cunningham, quoted in *Woman Talk* (Michele Brown and Ann O'Connor)

'The women in my family went to Australia to get away from the men,' she [Mick Jagger's mother] said.

Stanley Booth, *The True Adventures of the Rolling Stones*

When it comes to women, modern men are idiots. They don't know what they want, and so they never want, permanently,

60

what they get. They want a cream cake that is at the same time ham and eggs and at the same time porridge. They are fools. If only women weren't bound by fate to play up to them.

> **D. H. Lawrence,** *Selected Essays*

Being a woman is a terribly difficult trade, since it consists principally of dealing with men.

> **Joseph Conrad,** quoted in *Treasury of Humorous Quotations* (Esar)

My mother used to say it was a great relief to her being an old woman because men left her alone.

> **Jill Nicholls and Pat Moan,** *Spare Rib,* July 1978

Men don't understand, as a rule, that women like to get used to them by degrees.

> **John Oliver Hobbes,** quoted in *Macmillan Treasury of Relevant Quotations* (Edward F. Murphy)

Men are so silly. They don't—or won't—realize that it is not money, or clothes, or jewels their wives want, but tenderness, courtesy, understanding, and affection.

> **Marie Corelli,** quoted in *The Wit of Women* (L. and M. Cowan)

Men love things best; women love persons best.

> **Jean Paul,** quoted in *The Nuttall Dictionary of Quotations* (James Wood)

How men hate waiting while their wives shop for clothes and trinkets; how women hate waiting, often for much of their lives, while their husbands shop for fame and glory.

> **Thomas Szasz,** *The Second Sin*

Women's liberation is just a lot of foolishness. It's the men who are discriminated against. They can't bear children. And no one's likely to do anything about that.

Golda Meir, quoted in *Handbook of 20th Century Quotations* (Frank S. Pepper)

Men resent women because women bear kids, and seem to have this magic link with immortality that men lack. But they should stay home for a day with a kid; they'd change their minds.

Tuesday Weld, quoted in *A Book of Quotes* (Barbara Rowes), Dutton

. . . [soap operas] are the only place in our culture where grown-up men take seriously all the things that grown-up women have to deal with all day long.

Gloria Steinem, 'Night Thoughts of a Media Watcher', from *Outrageous Acts and Everyday Rebellions*

The traditional figures of revolution, Rousseau, Karl Marx, Lenin and others were no great emancipators of women and were themselves chauvinist. They left their wives slaving over a hot stove.

Sally Oppenheim, 'Sayings of the Week', *Observer*, 14th June 1981

Men *would* support us [the feminists] we are told, if only we learned how to ask for their support in the right way. It's a subtle and effective way of blaming the victim.

Gloria Steinem, *Outrageous Acts and Everyday Rebellions*

Lesbian is a label invented by the man to throw at any woman who dares to be his equal, who dares to challenge his prerogatives . . . who dares to assert the primacy of her own needs.

Radicalesbians, *The Woman-Identified Woman*, Radical Feminism

Cock of the walk, he took the choicest fodder,
and he was totem stud and constable
Until his comb and spurs were frozen, bled,
and then the hens, quite calmly, picked him dead

Alden Nowlan, 'Hens'

There aren't any hard women, just soft men.

Raquel Welch, quoted in *Woman Talk*
(Michele Brown and Ann O'Connor)

The only problem with women is men.

Kathie Sarachild, quoted in *Dictionary of*
Contemporary Quotations (Jonathon
Green)

'I once knew a man who was stabbed to death by a woman,' he
says. 'It gave him the surprise of his life.' 'I once knew a woman
who was beaten to death by a man,' she answers. 'I don't think
it surprised her in the least.'

From *The Duellists*

Fighting is essentially a masculine idea; a woman's weapon is
her tongue.

Hermione Gingold, quoted in *A Book of*
Quotes (Barbara Rowes), Dutton

Women like the simple things in life—like men.

Graffito in Chorlton-cum-Hardy ladies,
quoted in *Graffiti: The Scrawl of the Wild*
(Roger Kilroy)

Nothing contrasts more sharply with the masculine image of self-
confidence, rationality and control, than men's sulky, obtuse and
often virtually total dependence on their wives to articulate and
deal with their own unhappy feelings, and their own insensitiv-

ity, fear and passivity in helping their wives to deal with theirs.

Marc Feigen Fasteau, *The Male Machine*,
McGraw-Hill

A man may have a home and a family, love, companionship, domesticity and fatherhood, yet remain an active citizen of his age and country . . . a woman must 'choose'.

Charlotte Perkins Gilman (1906),
quoted in *Ms*, June 1973

All men are not slimy warthogs. Some men are silly giraffes, some woebegone puppies, some insecure frogs. But if one is not careful, those slimy warthogs can ruin it for all the others.

Cynthia Heimel, 'When In Doubt Say
No', *Ms*, February 1984

Never despise what it says in the women's magazines: it may not be subtle, but neither are men.

Zsa Zsa Gabor, 'Sayings of the Week',
Observer, 11th April, 1976

You see an awful lot of smart guys with dumb women, but you hardly ever see a smart woman with a dumb guy.

Erica Jong, quoted in *A Book of Quotes*
(Barbara Rowes), Dutton

Women prefer men who have something tender about them—especially the legal kind.

Kay Ingram, quoted in *Quotations for Our
Time* (Dr. Laurence Peter)

MEN, And Women

It is men who face the biggest problems in the future, adjusting to their new and complicated role.

Anna Ford, 'Sayings of the Week',
Observer, 4th January, 1981

A man who has nothing to do with women is always incomplete.

Cyril Connolly, *The Unquiet Grave*

MEN

Attitudes to Sex of

A woman is a woman until the day she dies, but a man's a man only as long as he can.

Moms Mabley, quoted in *Peter's Quotations* (Dr. Laurence Peter), Morrow

Give a man a free hand and he'll run it all over you.

Mae West, quoted in *Dictionary of Contemporary Quotations* (Jonathon Green)

You come out of a woman and you spend the rest of your life trying to get back inside.

Heathcote Williams, *Ibid.*

Among men, sex sometimes results in intimacy; among women, intimacy sometimes results in sex.

D. Symons, *The Evolution of Human Sexuality*

. . . The cultural impasse that early divides the sexes and prefigures their antagonism; woman's personal quest for a great love, and man's impersonal quest for a good lay.

Molly Haskell, 'Rape Fantasy', *Ms*, November 1976

PICKING ON MEN

One puzzling thing about men—they allow their sex instinct to drive them to where their intelligence never would take them.

> **Joan Fontaine,** quoted in *Bartlett's*
> *Unfamiliar Quotations* (Leonard Louis
> Levinson)

Guys can have head-on collisions with Greyhound buses—fifty people laying dead on the highway—and on the way to the hospital the guy makes a play for the nurse.

> **Lenny Bruce**

The most interesting man is the one who is not an easy lay.

> **Jackie Collins,** 'Sayings of the Week',
> *Observer*, 13th January, 1980

All too many men still seem to believe, in a rather naive and egocentric way, that what feels good to them is automatically what feels good to women.

> **Shere Hite,** quoted in *A Book of Quotes*
> (Barbara Rowes), Dutton

Fifty per cent of the women in this country are not having orgasms. If that were true of the male population, it would be declared a national emergency.

> **Margo St. James,** *San Francisco Bay*
> *Guardian*, 1978

We always seem to be having sex not so much for the sake of sex as to prove something. We reduce it almost to the level of a competitive sport. We talk about a man 'making a conquest' of a woman.

Andrew Goodman, *A Book About Men*
(Andrew Goodman and Patricia Welby)

You men are like cocks, you never make love,
but you clap your wings, and crow when you have done.

John Dryden, *Marriage à la Mode*

Aristocrats spend their childhood being beaten by fierce nannies
and their later years murdering wildlife, so it's hardly surprising
their sex lives are a bit cock-eyed.

Jilly Cooper, *Men and Superman*

However much men say sex is not on their minds all the time, it
is most of the time.

Jackie Collins, 'Sayings of the Week',
Observer, 19th July, 1984

Male sexual response is far brisker and more automatic; it is trig-
gered easily by things, like putting a quarter in a vending machine.

Alex Comfort, MD, quoted in *A Book of
Quotes* (Barbara Rowes), Dutton

Once you know what women are like, men get kind of boring.
I'm not trying to put them down, I mean I like them sometimes
as people, but sexually they're dull.

Rita Mae Brown, quoted in *A Book of
Quotes* (Barbara Rowes), Dutton

. . . some men, and particularly those who act like chauvinist
chest-thumpers, simply can't deal with passion in a woman. An
intense response to love-making threatens their precarious,
though much-flaunted, masculinity.

Anon, as told to Constance Bogan, *Cosmopolitan,* October 1972

'Gary has just two responses, when I tell him I want to be held,'
Pam says. ' "No", or "Sex". Sometimes I think he's a penis
walking around with a body attached.'

Barry Whit, *Making Love: A Man's Guide, 1984*

PICKING ON MEN

If Boys are Better, why should a male choose to love an inferior female? If a penis is so great, two penises should be even greater. In large and small ways, boys are actually conditioned against heterosexuality because society is so relentlessly 'for' masculinity.

Letty Cottin Pogrebin, *Ms,* October 1980

Men are weak and constantly need reassurance, so now that they fail to find adulation in the opposite sex, they're turning to each other. Less and less do men need women. More and more do gentlemen prefer gentlemen.

Anita Loos, *Kiss Hollywood Goodbye,* 1974

We are living in a male homosexual culture—Wall Street, the Vatican, football teams, fashion designers. Men are separatists, and they don't want women around for longer than it takes to screw them.

Phyllis Chesler, *About Men,* Simon & Schuster, 1978

What most men desire is a virgin who is a whore.

Edward Dahlberg, *Reasons of the Heart,* Horizon Press, New York

Inside every pornographer there is an infant screaming for the breast from which it has been torn. Pornography represents an endless and infinitely repeated effort to recapture that breast, and the bliss it offered.

Steven Marcus, *The Other Victorians*

It's a gentleman's trip. A man propositions you, a man busts you, a man judges you, a man jails you, and a man bails you out.

Lucia (a prostitute), speech on prostitution to Coyote Convention, June 1974, quoted in *Woman Talk* (Michele Brown and Ann O'Connor)

MEN, Attitudes to Sex of

Women would not be prostitutes if it were not for men.

Baroness Vickers, 'Sayings of the Week',
Observer, 3rd July, 1977

Dirty old men are incapable of being corrupted any further, and as long as they make up the majority of regular customers a bookseller does not break the law in selling dirty books to them, two High Court Judges decided yesterday.

Daily Telegraph, quoted in *Punch* by Alan
Coren, 23rd February, 1972

. . . men believe . . . that death is the dirty secret of sex.

Andrea Dworkin, *Pornography*, Putnam

MEN

Attitude to Contraception of

All males should deposit their sperm in a sperm bank and then present themselves for compulsory vasectomy. In future all children would be conceived by artificial insemination, thus ensuring a responsible attitude to planned parenthood and eliminating unwanted pregnancies. Try to get this on to the Statute Book and I confidently expect to be deafened by the sound of men demanding their right to choose.

Letter to the editor of *The Standard*, 6th February, 1985

Until that day when women, and only women, shall determine which American males must, by law, have vasectomies, then—and only then—will you or any man have the right to determine which American women can have abortions.

Betty Beale, quoted in *Ms*, March 1982

If men could get pregnant, abortion would be a sacrament.

Irish Woman Cab Driver, quoted in *Outrageous Acts and Everyday Rebellions* (Gloria Steinem)

PICKING ON MEN

With almost all doctors, population experts and drug manufacturers male, is it really a surprise that oral contraceptives were designed for women to take and men to promote?

Ellen Frankfort, quoted in *Woman Talk*
(Michele Brown and Ann O'Connor)

MEN

Constancy of

Sigh no more, ladies, sigh no more,
Men were deceivers ever,
One foot in sea and one on shore,
To one thing constant never.

> **William Shakespeare,** *Much Ado About*
> *Nothing*

Trust not a man; we are by nature false,
Dissembling, subtle, cruel and unconstant.

> **Thomas Otway,** *The Orphan*
> (seventeenth-century play)

I will believe in anything rather than in any man's constancy.

> **Montaigne,** quoted in *Macmillan Treasury*
> *of Relevant Quotations* (Edward F. Murphy)

Men are men; the best sometimes forget.

> **William Shakespeare,** *Othello*

Men's vows are women's traitors.

> **William Shakespeare,** *Cymbeline*

PICKING ON MEN

When a man talks of love, with caution trust him;
But if he swears, he'll certainly deceive thee.

Thomas Otway, *The Orphan*

All the vows that ever man have broke,
In number more than ever women spoke.

William Shakespeare, *A Midsummer
Night's Dream*

Man soon tires of mere beauty. In fact man, the inconstant, soon
tires of mere anything.

Arnold Haultain, *Hints for Lovers,*
Constable, 1910

'Men are always unfaithful to women in one way or another,'
Sheila said . . . 'If a man doesn't betray you it's probably because he can't.'

Joyce Carol Oates, *Solstice*

When a man wants to deceive you, he'll find a way of escape
through the tiniest of holes.

Colette, quoted in *The Wit of Women*
(L. and M. Cowan)

Our Aunts and Grandmothers allwaies tell us Men are a sort of
Animals, that if ever they are constant 'tis only where they are
ill us'd. 'Twas a kind of Paradox I could never believe. Experience has taught me the truth of it.

Lady Mary Wortley Montagu, quoted in
Macmillan Dictionary of Relevant Quotations
(Edward F. Murphy)

Man's not worth a moment's pain,
Base, ungrateful, fickle, vain.

James Grainger, 'Ode to Solitude'

MEN

Social Graces of

A healthy male adult bore consumes each year one and a half times his own weight in other people's patience.

John Updike, *Confessions of a Wild Bore*

The man who suspects his own tediousness is yet to be born.

Thomas Bailey Aldrich, *Leaves from a Notebook,*
quoted in *International Thesaurus of Quotations*
(Rhoda Thomas Tripp), Penguin

There is a moment when a man develops enough confidence and ease in a relationship to bore you to death.

Eve Babitz, 'Slow Days, Fast Company',
1977

Men get opinions as boys learn to spell.
By reiteration chiefly.

Elizabeth Barrett Browning, 'Aurora
Leigh'

A man is like a phonograph with half a dozen records.
You soon get tired of them all.

George Bernard Shaw, quoted in *Who
Said That?* (Renie Gee)

PICKING ON MEN

Men will pay large sums to whores
For telling them they are not bores.

> **W. H. Auden,** 'New Year Letter', *Collected Poems*

No healthy male ever really thinks or talks of anything save himself.

> **H. L. Mencken**

I've found that men who talk a lot are doing what they do best.

> **Anon**

Blessed is the man who, having nothing to say, abstains from giving wordy evidence of the fact.

> **George Eliot,** *Theophrastus Such*

Women like silent men. They think they're listening.

> **Marcel Achard,** quoted in *International Thesaurus of Quotations* (Rhoda Thomas Tripp), Penguin

Men have an unusual talent for making a bore out of everything they touch.

> **Yoko Ono,** quoted in *Woman Talk* (Michele Brown and Ann O'Connor)

Every hero becomes a bore at last.

> **Ralph Waldo Emerson,** *Uses of Great Men*

When he said we were trying to make a fool of him, I could only murmur that the Creator had beaten us to it.

> **Ilka Chase,** quoted in *Violets and Vinegar* (Jilly Cooper and Tom Hartman)

Most of us, though we are bidden to look forward to an eternity of calm fruition, cannot spend an evening without trying to escape from a gentleman whom we know slightly and find, it seems, an intolerable bore—ourselves.

> **Dean Inge,** quoted in *Penguin Dictionary of Modern Quotations* (J. M. and M. J. Cohen)

A man by himself is in bad company.

> **Eric Hoffer,** quoted in *The Book of Unusual Quotations* (Rudolph Flesch), Cassell

One might ask why any man who cannot bear his own company for half an hour should be acceptable to anyone else on a 24-hour basis . . .

> **Beata Bishop with Pat McNeill,** *Below the Belt*

The minute a man is convinced that he is interesting, he is not.

> **Stephen Leacock,** quoted in *Bartlett's Unfamiliar Quotations* (Leonard Louis Levinson)

Some men are born mediocre, some men achieve mediocrity, and some men have mediocrity thrust upon them.

> **Joseph Heller,** quoted in *Dictionary of Contemporary Quotations* (Jonathon Green)

Some men think they have an inferiority complex when, as a matter of fact, they are just inferior.

> **Jacob M. Braude,** *Speaker's Encyclopaedia*, Prentice-Hall

There are a sort of men whose visages
Do cream and mantle like a standing pond,
And do a willful stillness entertain,
With purpose to be dressed in an opinion

of wisdom, gravity, profound conceit;
As who would say, 'I am Sir Oracle,
And when I ope my lips let no dog bark.'

William Shakespeare, *The Merchant of Venice*

What do you expect from a pig but a grunt.

Anon

The softer a man's head the louder his socks.

Helen Rowland, quoted in *Treasury of
Humorous Quotations* (Esar)

Men are contented to be laughed at for their wit but not for their
folly.

Jonathan Swift, quoted in *The Nuttall
Dictionary of Quotations* (James Wood)

I fear nothing so much as a man who is witty all day long.

Mme de Sevigné, quoted in *Violets and
Vinegar* (Jilly Cooper and Tom Hartman)

Men who have been famous for their looks have never been famous for anything else.

Arthur Ponsonby, quoted in *Macmillan
Treasury of Relevant Quotations* (Edward F. Murphy)

. . . the types who make passes at girls who wear glasses—so
they can see themselves in the reflection.

Stephanie Calman, *Gentlemen Prefer My Sister*

The sexual revolution began with Man's discovery that he was
not attractive to Woman, as such. The lion had his mane, the
peacock his gorgeous plumage, but Man found himself in a three-
button sack suit.

E. B. White, quoted in *Cassell's Book of
Humorous Quotations*

Never trust a man whose tie is habitually an inch below his collar.

> Letter to *The Times*, quoted in 'Sayings of the Week', *Observer*, 5th July, 1981

No man is a hero to his valet.

> **Anne Bigot de Cornuel,** quoted in *Woman Talk* (Michele Brown and Ann O'Connor)

The man who is always the life of the party will be the death of his wife.

> **Fred Sparks,** *Saturday Review*, 5th December, 1964

It is possible that blondes also prefer gentlemen.

> **Mamie van Doren,** quoted in *Woman Talk* (Michele Brown and Ann O'Connor)

Women speak because they wish to speak, whereas a man speaks only when driven to speech by something outside himself—like, for instance, he can't find any clean socks.

> **Jean Kerr,** *The Snake Has All the Lines*

Chivalry: a man's inclination to defend a woman against every man but himself.

> **Anon**

On the second night of his visit, our distinguished guest [Sir Charles Dilke] met Laura in the passage on her way to bed; he said to her: 'If you will kiss me, I will give you a signed photograph of myself.' To which she answered: 'It's awfully good of you, Sir Charles, but I would rather not, for what on earth should I do with the photograph?'

> **Margot Asquith,** quoted in *Violets and Vinegar* (Jilly Cooper and Tom Hartman)

Conceit is God's gift to little men.

> **Bruce Barton,** quoted in *Handbook of*
> *20th Century Quotations* (Frank S. Pepper)

I don't believe men have the faintest idea why their ghastly gallant little gestures can make women so angry they could choke . . . What makes us hopping mad is the assumption . . . that the poor little addle-pated lady will be so overcome with all the gallantry that she won't even see what the big, crafty men are up to. Like hell she won't; she'll just be crosser than a wet cat that you thought she was so easily bamboozled.

> **Katharine Whitehorn,** 'Living', *Observer*,
> 6th January, 1980

Virginia Cowle's Black List of Men:
Men, who take you to a musical comedy and entertain you by commenting ecstatically on the figures of the chorus.

Men, who tell you how wonderful it is to meet a woman with a mind—then give your hand a squeeze.

Men, who inform you that only men are capable of enduring friendship.

Men, who break off in the middle of a story with a gallant smirk, announcing that the refining presence of a woman does not permit them to continue.

Men, who when rebuffed inform you that you must be suffering from some strange Freudian complex.

Men, who spend the evening telling you how divine you are, then fail to call you up for a week.

Men, who spend the evening telling you how divine someone else is.

> **Virginia Cowle,** quoted in *The Wit of Women* (L. and M. Cowan)

The true male never yet walked
Who liked to listen when his mate talked.

> **Anne Wickham,** 'The Affinity', quoted in *Violets and Vinegar* (Jilly Cooper and Tom Hartman)

No man would listen to you talk if he didn't know it was his turn next.

> **Ed Howe,** quoted in *Quotations for Our Time* (Dr. Laurence Peter)

Men have to do some awfully mean things to keep up their respectability.

> **George Bernard Shaw,** quoted in *Encyclopedia of Practical Quotations* (Hoyt), Funk & Wagnalls

It took millions of years to make men out of monkeys, but sometimes it takes only a few minutes to reverse the process.

> **Jacob M. Braude,** *Speaker's Encyclopaedia,* Prentice-Hall

As there are some flowers which you should smell but slightly to extract all that is pleasant in them . . . so there are some men with whom a slight acquaintance is quite sufficient to draw out all that is agreeable; a more intimate one would be unsafe and unsatisfactory.

> **Walter Savage Landor,** *Between Friends*

Few men—and women—are perceptive enough to distinguish between the man who stands alone because he's independent, and the man who stands alone because he can't get on with people.

As a rule that's what the Loner's secret boils down to . . . more often than not he's only strong and silent because he has nothing to say.

Beata Bishop with Pat McNeill, *Below the Belt*

If a man be discreet enough to take to hard drinking in his youth, before his general emptiness is ascertained, his friends invariably credit him with a host of shining qualities which, we are given to understand, lie baulked and frustrated by his one unfortunate weakness.

Agnes Repplier, *A Plea for Humour,* quoted in
Woman Talk (Michele Brown and Ann O'Connor)

Many a man's reputation would not know his character if they met on the street.

Elbert Hubbard, quoted in *Bartlett's
Unfamiliar Quotations* (Leonard Louis Levinson)

I couldn't just tell him to push off. He was so revolting I felt sorry for him. That's why the most unattractive men are the vainest—they're carried along by the pity of women.

Overheard on a bus

A good dog is so much a nobler beast than an indifferent man that one sometimes gladly exchanges the society of one for that of the other.

Sir William Butler, *Wild North Land* (1873)

Nobody talks more of free enterprise and competition and of the best man winning than the man who inherited his father's store or farm.

C. Wright Mills, quoted in *Quotations for
Our Time* (Dr. Laurence Peter)

MEN, Social Graces of

I have had pipe smoke in my eyes for twenty years.
Lady Falkender, 'Sayings of the Week',
Observer, 13th February, 1977

With men he can be rational and unaffected, but when he has ladies to please, every feature works.
Jane Austen, Mr. Knightly of Mr. Elton, *Emma*

The trouble with self-made men is that they quit the job too early.
Herbert V. Prochnow and Herbert V.
Prochnow Jr., *The Public Speaker's Treasure Chest*

The trouble with self-made men is that they're working with inferior materials.
Anon

A self-made man tends to worship his creator.
Anon

Some men are self-made, others the revised work of women.
Anon

Beware of men who refer to other men as 'boys'.
Richard J. Needham, *A Friend in Needham*, Macmillan, 1969

The Club. One of the last bastions of male chauvinism. Not only do they discriminate against women but also against each other.
Jilly Cooper, *Men and Supermen*

Clubs are places where men spend all their time thinking angrily about nothing.
Viscount Castlerosse, *Lord Castlerosse,
His Life and Times* (George Malcolm Thomson)

PICKING ON MEN

The more I see of men, the more I like dogs.

Mme de Staël, quoted in *Violets and Vinegar* (Jilly Cooper and Tom Hartman)

MEN

In Friendship

Despite the time men spend together, their contact rarely goes beyond the external, a limitation which tends to make their friendship shallow and unsatisfying.

Marc Feigen Fasteau, *The Male Machine,*
McGraw-Hill

One waits a long time for a male friend.

Eleanor Perry, *Ms,* November 1976

You can be the best of friends with a man, and then you get married and right away he's different.

Barbara Hutton

MEN

In Sickness

The devil was sick, the devil a monk would be;
The devil was well, the devil a monk was he.

> **Rabelais,** quoted in *Stokes Cyclopaedia of Familiar Quotations* (Treffry)

Why is it that men who can go through severe accidents, air raids and any other major crisis always seem to think they are at death's door when they have a simple head cold?

> **Shirley Booth,** *Ladies' Home Journal,* November 1943

Gout is very much in my line, gentleman are not.

> Letter from **Dr. Elizabeth Garrett Anderson,** in reply to a gent hoping to be treated for gout, quoted in *Dear Sir, Drop Dead!* (Donald Carroll)

MEN

At Work

I have yet to hear a man ask for advice on how to combine marriage and a career.

Gloria Steinem, LBC radio interview, 2nd April, 1984

A woman's work is never done by men.

Anon

The average male gets his living by such depressing devices that boredom becomes a sort of natural state to him.

H. L. Mencken, *In Defence of Women*

The Actor

Some of my best leading men have been dogs and horses.

Elizabeth Taylor, interviewed by John
Higgins in *The Times*, 18th February, 1981

An actor is a guy who, if you aren't talking about him, isn't listening.

Marlon Brando, 'Sayings of the Week',
Observer, January 1956

91

PICKING ON MEN

No good actor is ever wholly masculine: something, some vocal or physical trait, betrays his debt to womankind, the debt which every man owes, but which most of us, out of some primitive animosity, do our best to hide.

Kenneth Tynan, *He That Plays the King*

The Bank Robber

Johnnie's just an ordinary fellow. Of course he goes out and holds up banks and things, but he's really just like any other fellow, aside from that.

Mary Kinder, in *Dillinger, A Short and Violent Life* (Robert Cromie), quoted in *Woman Talk* (Michele Brown and Ann O'Connor)

The Boss

Men are never so tired and harassed as when they have to deal with a woman who wants a raise.

Michael Korda, *Male Chauvinism—How It Works*

Few bosses would tell a male clerk to brew up a pot of tea.

John Forrester, 'Sayings of the Week', *Observer*, 23rd May, 1976

Korda is damningly good on the male hierarchy's mean little ways of keeping women in their place. He notes the gimmick of coming into a room with your arm round a woman saying: 'Now I want you all to know that this is Jane's own project.' It *is* her project, but put that way they think he's being gallant—and he can still disclaim it if it's a flop.

Katherine Whitehorn, reviewing Michael Korda's *Power in the Office* in the *Observer*, 28th March, 1976

92

MEN, At Work

An office party is not, as is sometimes supposed, the Managing Director's chance to kiss the tea girl. It is the tea girl's chance to kiss the Managing Director (however bizarre an ambition this may seem to anyone who has seen the Managing Director face on).

Katherine Whitehorn, quoted in *Violets and Vinegar* (Jilly Cooper and Tom Hartman)

The Builder

It's 'aving 'ouses built by men, I believe, makes all the work and trouble.

H. G. Wells, *Kipps*

The Censor

A censor is a man who knows more than he thinks you ought to.

Dr. Laurence Peter, *Quotations for Our Time*

The Churchman

A clergyman has nothing to do but to be slovenly and selfish— read the newspaper, watch the weather, and quarrel with his wife. His curate does all the work and the business of his own life is to dine.

Jane Austen, *Mansfield Park*

My friends point out that a half-witted man can take round a collecting bag, but that the most brilliant women must have no part in the church.

The Bishop of Woolwich, Dr. John Robinson, quoted in *The Wit of the Church* (Michael Bateman and Shirley Stenning)

When you go to a church where two men stand behind the Communion table, and ten men serve Communion, and another man stands at the lectern and reads the scripture, and another man stands up and preaches, and three more men stand in the aisle handing out bulletins, you hear a fairly loud statement about the nature of the Church.

The Rev. Harold Dowler, quoted in *Ms,*
March 1982

The Competition

Men are vain, but they won't mind women working so long as they get smaller salaries for the same job.

Irwin Shrewsbury Cobb, quoted in *Treasury of*
Humorous Quotations (Esar)

Men, having kept work as their exclusive preserve for so long, *are* defensive with the women who try to enter it, and show a strong tendency to shunt us into the more traditional female roles—not managing director, but his PA; not headmaster, but deputy; not sales, but personnel, and so on.

Cathy Douglas, *The Superwoman Trap*

We must make the utmost use of those qualities which men often blatantly lack—and which businesses and administrative departments everywhere desperately need—our in-built tact, patience and perseverance.

Harriet Crawley, 'Women in Top Jobs',
Cosmopolitan, August 1972

In many professions it seems to me that women have to be that much cleverer or stronger than men. But luckily this is often so.

Naomi Mitchison, 'Growing Pains',
Guardian, 23rd October, 1984

Whatever women do they must do twice as well as men to be thought half as good. Luckily this is not difficult.

Charlotte Whitton, quoted in *Liberty*, 1962

The Executive

Men are such duds, you know. They take themselves so seriously. They mumble on for hours with their noses in a sheaf of papers.

Mary Kay, interviewed by Jeremy
Campbell in *The Standard*, August 29th, 1984

My daddy doesn't work, he just goes to the office; but sometimes he does errands on the way home.

Anon, *Ladies' Home Journal*, November 1946

The surest way to get a thing done is to give it to the busiest man you know, and he'll have his secretary do it.

Anon, quoted in *Bartlett's Unfamiliar
Quotations* (Leonard Louis Levinson)

I have a modest proposal for anyone who maintains that 'he' is just plain easier: since 'he' has been the style for several centuries now—and since it really includes everybody, anyway, right?—it seems only fair to give 'she' a turn . . . And don't be upset by the business letter that begins 'Dear Madam,' fellas. It means you, too.

Lindsy Van Gelder, *Ms*, April 1980

PICKING ON MEN

The Explorer

Civilized men arrived in the Pacific, armed with alcohol, syphilis, trousers, and the Bible.

> **Havelock Ellis,** quoted in *Handbook of 20th Century Quotations* (Frank S. Pepper)

The Pilgrim Fathers have much to answer for. I have read that when they landed in America they fell upon their knees; then they fell upon the aborigines.

> **John Foster Fraser,** *Round the World on a Wheel,* Thomas Nelson & Sons, 1899

The Manual Worker

You can always tell a British workman by his hands. They are always in his pockets.

> Graffito, reported on BBC Radio 4, 'Quote Unquote', 26th June, 1980, quoted in *Handbook of 20th Century Quotations* (Frank S. Pepper)

The Obstetrician

Delivering a baby is the ultimate male ego trip.

> **Barbara Seaman,** *New York Post,* 28th September, 1973

The Photographer

Armies of men, herds really, with cameras at the ready, stampeded . . . to observe sweet-natured, patient women whose bodies are shaped in a manner that you hardly ever see in the courses of normal life. Fat, balding, ugly, drunken, uncouth and deeply unattractive men with flashlights tell these exquisite women what to do and the women do it.

Stephen Pile, on topless models promoting motorbikes, *Sunday Times*, 28th October, 1984

The Pirate

Gentlemen of fortune . . . usually trust little among themselves, and right they are.

R. L. Stevenson, *Treasure Island*

The Policeman

I have never seen a situation so dismal that a policeman couldn't make it worse.

Brendan Behan, quoted in *A Book of Quotes* (Barbara Rowes), Dutton

The Politician

A politician is an arse upon which everyone has sat except a man.

e. e. cummings, quoted in *Handbook of 20th Century Quotations* (Frank S. Pepper)

PICKING ON MEN

One of the things that politics has taught me is that men are not a reasoned or reasonable sex.

Margaret Thatcher, in conversation with
Anthony King, BBC Radio 4, 14th January, 1972

My family would hardly approve of my marrying a politician.

Joan Fontaine, to Adlai Stevenson quoted in
Handbook of 20th Century Quotations (Frank S. Pepper)

Mothers all want their sons to grow up to become President, but they don't want them to become politicians in the process.

John F. Kennedy, quoted in *A Book of
Quotes* (Barbara Rowes), Dutton

In politics, if you want anything said, ask a man; if you want anything done, ask a woman.

Margaret Thatcher, quoted in *The Changing
Anatomy of Britain* (Anthony Sampson)

For Hon. Members opposite the deterrent is a phallic symbol. It convinces them that they are men.

George Wigg, MP, quoted in *Penguin
Dictionary of Modern Quotations* (J. M. and M. J. Cohen)

A politician is a statesman who approaches every question with an open mouth.

Adlai Stevenson, quoted in *The Fine Art
of Political Wit* (L. Harris)

They say women talk too much. If you have worked in congress you know that the filibuster was invented by men.

Clare Booth Luce, quoted in *Dictionary
of Contemporary Quotations* (Jonathon Green)

Families, when a child is born
Want it to be intelligent.

MEN, At Work

I, through intelligence,
Having wrecked my whole life,
Only hope the baby will prove
Ignorant and stupid.
Then he will crown a tranquil life
By becoming a Cabinet Minister.

> **Su Tung-po,** 'On The Birth of his Son'
> (trans. Sir Arthur Waley), *170 Chinese Poems*

I know what a statesman is. He is a dead politician. We need more statesmen.

> **Robert C. Edwards** (attrib.), quoted in
> *Canadian Dictionary of Quotations and
> Phrases* (Robert M. Hamilton and Dorothy
> Shields)

The Publisher

'My most recent mistake was turning down *Man's Best Friend*. It's a cartoon book about men's willies which has been at the top of the paperback lists for weeks. I didn't choose to publish it because I thought it was disgusting,' adds an indignant but peeved Blond, a Marks and Spencer heir. 'All the women in the office wanted to accept it and the men didn't. We won.'

> **Anthony Blond,** 'Londoner's Diary', *The
> Standard*, 4th February, 1985

The Salesman

The superior man understands what is right; the inferior man understands what will sell.

> **Confucius**

PICKING ON MEN

The Skiver

Men build bridges and throw railroads across deserts, and yet they contend successfully that the job of sewing on a button is beyond them. Accordingly, they don't have to sew buttons.

Heywood Broun, quoted in *International Thesaurus of Quotations* (Rhonda Thomas Tripp), Penguin

The Soldier

When the military man approaches, the world locks up its spoons and packs off its womankind.

George Bernard Shaw, *Man and Superman*

The Teacher

He who can, does. He who cannot teaches.

George Bernard Shaw, *Education*

The Technocrat

Technological man can't believe in anything that can't be measured, taped, put in a computer.

Clare Booth Luce, quoted in *Woman Talk* (Michele Brown and Ann O'Connor)

The Tycoon

If all the rich men in the world divided up their money amongst themselves there wouldn't be enough to go round.

Christina Stead, quoted in *Penguin Dictionary of Modern Quotations* (J. M. and M. J. Cohen)

MEN

At Sport

Billie Jean King said today she let male tennis players win against her 'to spare injuring their fragile egos'.

Billie Jean King, quoted in *The Standard*,
12th September, 1984

Men don't like playing women. For example if I'm playing in a money competition, everybody has to pay the same amount to enter, but if you win and beat a man he'll say 'Oh, I just can't play a woman' . . . any old excuse!

Mina Jones, 'Think Darts', interview by
Fiona Green, *Spare Rib*, February 1979

We have nothing against men cricketers. Some of them are quite nice people, even though they don't win as often as we do.

Rachel Heyhoe Flint, 'Sayings of the
Week', *Observer*, 21st December, 1975

[Footballers are] . . . miry gladiators whose sole purpose in life is to position a surrogate human head between two poles.

Elizabeth Hogg, *Daily Telegraph*, 7th
September, 1979

PICKING ON MEN

When a man wants to murder a tiger he calls it sport; when a tiger wants to murder him he calls it ferocity.

George Bernard Shaw

Hi! Handsome hunting man
Fire your little gun.
Bang! Now the animal
Is dead and dumb and done
Never more to peep again, creep again, leap again
Eat or sleep or drink again, oh what fun.

Walter de la Mare, 'The Huntsman'

MEN

Nice

A nice man is a man of nasty ideas.

Jonathan Swift, *Thoughts on Various Subjects*

No nice men are good at getting taxis—Whitehorn's Second Law.

Katharine Whitehorn, *Observer,* January 1977

MEN

Great

Great men are almost always bad men, even when they exercise influence and not authority.

J. E. E. Dalberg (1st Baron Acton),
quoted in *Quotations in History* (Alan and
Veronica Palmer)

A big man has no time really to do anything but just sit and be big.

F. Scott Fitzgerald, *This Side of Paradise*

The greatest men of the past were all masters of Humbug, and so are the greatest men today.

Sir W. Van Horne, letter of 1909, quoted
in *Dictionary of Canadian Quotations and
Phrases* (Robert M. Hamilton and Dorothy
Shields)

The two maxims of any great man at court are—always to keep his countenance and never to keep his word.

Jonathan Swift, quoted in *Bartlett's
Unfamiliar Quotations* (Leonard Louis
Levinson)

PICKING ON MEN

Great men are absolutely splendid in wartime, but they can be dangerous in peacetime, for great men, powerful men, have produced wars, as Napoleon did.

A. J. P. Taylor, 'Sayings of the Week',
Observer, 21st August, 1977

The banalities of great men pass for wit.

Alexander Chase, quoted in *Handbook of
20th Century Quotations* (Frank S. Pepper)

There are no great men, buster. There are only men.

Elaine Stewart, in *The Bad and the
Beautiful*, screenplay **Charles Schnee**,
based on short stories by **George Bradshaw**,
quoted in *Dictionary of Contemporary
Quotations* (Jonathon Green)

MEN

National Types of

The American

The American male is the world's fattest and softest; this might explain why he also loves guns—you can always get your revolver up.

> **Gore Vidal,** *Matters of Fact and Fiction*

The typical successful American businessman was born in the country, where he worked like hell so he could live in the City, where he worked like hell so he could live in the country.

> **Don Marquis,** quoted in *Macmillan Treasury of Relevant Quotations* (Edward F. Murphy)

It is a curious fact that you can give an American man some kind of a ball and he will be thoroughly content.

> **Judson P. Phillips,** quoted in *Macmillan Treasury of Relevant Quotations* (Edward F. Murphy)

They have wonderful minds. So much is stored inside—all those sports scores and so on.

> **Jane Seymour,** *Time,* 1980

American women expect to find in their husbands a perfection that English women only hope to find in their butlers.

> **Somerset Maugham,** *A Writer's Notebook*

PICKING ON MEN

American men say 'I love you' as part of the conversation.

Liv Ullmann, *Changing*

I have seen many American women who look like queens, but I have never seen an American man who looks like a king.

Count Hermann Keyserling, *Ladies'*
Home Journal, October 1946

. . . woman governs America because America is a land of boys who refuse to grow up.

Salvador de Madariaga, quoted in
Penguin Dictionary of Modern Quotations
(J. M. and M. J. Cohen)

The American male doesn't mature until he has exhausted all other possibilities.

Wilfred Sheed, *Office Politics,* quoted in
International Thesaurus of Quotations
(Rhoda Thomas Tripp), Penguin

I never saw an American man walk or stand well; they are nearly all hollow-chested and round-shouldered.

Frances Trollope, quoted in *Woman Talk*
(Michele Brown and Ann O'Connor)

The dream of the American male is for a female who has an essential languor which is not laziness, who is unaccompanied except by himself, and who does not let him down. He desires a beautiful, but comprehensible creature who does not destroy a perfect situation by forming a complete sentence.

E. B. White, *The Second Tree from the Corner*

With Phyllis Schlafly the suspicion one often has with American women—that they don't greatly admire American men—becomes a near-certainty: she thinks the reason the Congressmen passed the original ERA (Equal Rights Amendment) was that they were terrified of the feminists: 'they just came unglued'.

Katharine Whitehorn, *Observer,* 19th
October, 1980

The Brazilian

A recent crime survey in a Brazilian newspaper, in fact, showed that in 1980, in the City of São Paulo alone, several hundred women were put to death by their husbands or lovers. Few of those men were seriously punished for their actions.

Ms, March 1982

The British

He is white and male, forty and married, bourgeois and British— all items to anyone's contemporary discredit, as he knows perfectly well.

Malcolm Bradbury, *Rates of Exchange*

The Burmese

I asked a Burmese why women, after centuries of following their men, now walk ahead. He said there were many unexploded landmines since the war.

Robert Mueller, quoted in *Quotations for
Our Time* (Dr. Laurence Peter)

PICKING ON MEN

The Canadian

Men who are attractive to most women are rarities, in this country, at any rate. I think that it is because a man, to be attractive, must be free to give his whole time to it, and the Canadian male is so hounded by taxes and the rigours of our climate that he is lucky to be alive, without being irresistible as well.

Robertson Davies, *Table Talk of Samuel Marchbanke*

The Englishman

I know why the sun never sets on the British Empire; God wouldn't trust an Englishman in the dark.

Duncan Spaeth, quoted in *The Last Word*
(Gyles Brandreth)

The Englishman respects your opinions; but he never thinks of your feelings.

Sir Wilfrid Laurier, quoted in *Dictionary of Canadian Quotations and Phrases* (Robert M. Hamilton and Dorothy Shields)

It's not that the English man can't feel—it's that he is afraid to feel. He has been taught at his public school that feeling is bad form. He must not express great joy or sorrow, or even open his mouth too wide when he talks—his pipe might fall out if he did.

E. M. Forster, 'Notes on the English Character', *Abinger Harvest*

An English man thinks himself moral when he is only uncomfortable.

George Bernard Shaw, *Man and Superman*

Distinguished English gentlemen will happily walk around with flowers in their lapels, silk handkerchiefs in their overcoats, a wad of fivers in their Morocco wallets—and holes in their underwear.

Dennis Barker, *Guardian*, 20th January, 1970

An Englishman's social standing seems to depend on the number of people he can afford to despise.

Peter McArthur, *To Be Taken With Salt*

If you mean that noisiness and hysteria are proofs of unfitness for public life then every Parliament in the world should close, every election meeting be prohibited, every sex be disfranchised. Did Englishmen ever get their voting right save by noisiness and hysteria?

Israel Zangwill, letter to *The Times* on the Suffragette Movement, 29th October, 1906, quoted in *Handbook of 20th Century Quotations* (Frank S. Pepper)

One has often wondered whether upon the whole earth there is anything so unintelligent, so unapt to perceive how the world is really going, as an ordinary young Englishman of our upper class.

Matthew Arnold, *Culture and Anarchy*

The Englishman foxtrots as he fox-hunts, with all his being, through thickets, through ditches, over hedges, through chiffons, through waiters, over saxophones, to the victorious finish: and who goes home depends on how many the ambulance will accommodate.

Ella Wheeler Wilcox, quoted in *The Wit of Women* (L. and M. Cowan)

PICKING ON MEN

The Irishman

It might be marvellous to be a man—then I could stop worrying about what's fair to women and just cheerfully assume I was superior, and that they had all been born to iron my shirts. Better still, I could be an Irish man—then I would have all the privileges of being male without giving up the right to be wayward, temperamental and an appealing minority.

Katharine Whitehorn, *Observer*, 29th
June, 1980

The Italian

The Italian male appraises every female from sixteen to sixty (with the exception of his mother) for her potential in bed. The theory is that friendship between a man and a woman is impossible unless they have been lovers, for otherwise, what passes for *rapport* can only be sexual curiosity.

Luciana Avedon and Jeanne Moli, 'The
Italian Male', *Cosmopolitan*, July 1974

The Russian

'What's a typical Soviet man?' asked someone at the meeting at A Woman's Place in London. 'A sexist phallocrat,' was the succinct answer.

Tatiana Mamonova, 'Women and
Russia', *Spare Rib*, June 1981

The Westerner

The further he went West the more convinced he felt that the Wise Men came from the East.

Sydney Smith, quoted in *Who Said That?*
(Renie Gee)

The White Man

When a white man in Africa by accident looks into the eyes of a native and sees the human being (which it is his chief preoccupation to avoid), his sense of guilt, which he denies, fumes up in resentment and he brings down the whip.

Doris Lessing, *The Grass is Singing*

'All white men ain't dumb,' says Etta, 'just most of them.'

W. P. Kinsella, *The Moccasin Telegraph*,
Penguin Books, Canada, 1983

MEN

Proverbs Relating to

The birth of a man who thinks he's a god is no new thing.

Old female proverb

As an infant, man is wrapped in his mother's womb; grown-up he is wrapped in custom; dead he is wrapped in earth.

Malay proverb

If the best man's faults were written on his forehead it would make him pull his hat over his eyes.

Gaelic proverb

Adam must have an Eve to blame for his faults.

Italian proverb

Men are very generous with that which cost them nothing.

English proverb

Men apt to promises are apt to forget.

English proverb

When a rogue kisses you, count your teeth.

Hebrew proverb

PICKING ON MEN

The bachelor is a peacock, the engaged man a lion, and the married man a jackass.

German proverb

If you hear that a mountain has moved, believe; but if you hear that a man has changed his character, believe it not.

Muhammadan proverb

Fear the goat from the front, the horse from the rear, and man from all sides.

Russian proverb

MEN

Miscellaneous Insults to

Most men are in a coma when they are at rest and mad when they act.

Epicurus, Quoted in *International Thesaurus of Quotations* (Rhonda Thomas Tripp), Penguin

Ah, how unjust to nature and himself
Is thoughtless, thankless, inconsistent man!

Edward Young, quoted in *Quotations for Our Time* (Dr. Laurence Peter)

The magnificence of mountains, the serenity of nature—
nothing is safe from the idiot marks of man's passing.

Loudon Wainwright, *Ibid.*

Were I (who to my cost already am
One of those strange, prodigious creatures, man)
A spirit free to choose, for my own share,
What case of flesh and blood I planned to wear,
I'd be a dog, a monkey or a bear,
Or anything but that vain animal
Who is so proud of being Rational.

John Wilmont, Earl of Rochester, quoted in *Who Said That?* (Renie Gee)

PICKING ON MEN

To call man an animal is to flatter him; he's a machine, a walking dildo.

Valerie Solanas, *Scum Manifesto*,
Matriarchy Study Group

Men are like sheep, of which a flock is more easily driven than a single one.

Whateley, quoted in *The Nuttall Dictionary of Quotations* (James Wood)

You cannot make a man by standing a sheep on its hind legs: But by standing a flock of sheep in that position you can make a crowd of men.

Max Beerbohm, *Zuleika Dobson*

I wonder why men can get serious at all . . . If I were a man I would always be laughing at myself.

Yoko Ono, 'On Film No. 1' (1967),
Grapefruit. Reprinted *Ms*, October 1973

We men are mostly a hypocritical lot.

Anon, Letter in *Ms*, September 1972

I loathe all men; such unromantic creatures!
The coarsest tastes, and, ah! the coarsest features!
Betty!—the salts!—I'm sick with mere vexation,
To hear them called the Lords of the Creation:
They swear fierce oaths, they seldom say their prayers;
And then, they shed no tears,—unfeeling bears.

Winthrop Mackworth Praed, 'Prologue for the Honeymoon'

While woman remains nearer the infantile type, man approaches more to the senile. The extreme variational tendency of man expresses itself in a larger percentage of genius, insanity and idiocy; woman remains more nearly normal.

W. I. Thomas, quoted in *The Female Eunuch* (Germaine Greer)

A woman I have heard, takes to herself a mate and reproduces her kind, and is thereby complete; with a woman completion, I believe, signifies multiplication. As to a man, I doubt if even multiplication completes him; possibly nothing completes him; possibly he remains an imperfect creature to the end.

Rose Macauley, quoted in *Macmillan Treasury of Revelant Quotations* (Edward F. Murphy)

Men can be very odd.

Stephanie Calman, *Gentlemen Prefer My Sister*

Good wombs have born bad sons.

William Shakespeare, *The Tempest*

All men are bad, and in their badness reign.

William Shakespeare, *Sonnets*

There is no man so good, who, were he to submit all his thoughts and actions to the law, would not deserve hanging ten times in his life.

Montaigne

Men are in general so tricky, so envious, and so cruel, that when we find one who is only weak, we are too happy.

Voltaire, quoted in *The Nuttall Dictionary of Quotations* (James Wood)

Men blush less for their crimes than for their weaknesses and vanities.

La Bruyère, *Ibid.*

PICKING ON MEN

Well, time wounds all heels.

> **Jane Ace,** quoted in *Violets and Vinegar*
> (Jilly Cooper and Tom Hartman)

God made man, and then said I can do better than that and made woman.

> **Adela St John Rogers,** quoted in *A Book
> of Quotes* (Barbara Rowes), Dutton

The great power of a woman is her theatrical aspect, her mask, her sense of mystery. It is very rarely that you find men who have mystery.

> **Yves St Laurent,** 'Sayings of the Week',
> *Observer,* 10th April, 1977

We cannot reduce women to equality. Equality is a step down for most women.

> **Phyllis Schlafly,** *quoted in A Book of
> Quotes* (Barbara Rowes), Dutton

Men are always out for what they can get.

> **Alice Munro,** written on a postcard in
> 1968, quoted in *Dictionary of Canadian
> Quotations and Phrases* (Robert M.
> Hamilton and Dorothy Shields)

There are always men who will do things if the price is right.

> **Jennifer Potter,** *The Taking of Agnes*

The only original thing about some men is original sin.

> **Helen Rowland,** quoted in *Treasury of
> Humorous Quotations* (Esar)

There is only one grade of men; they are all contemptible.

> **E. W. Howe,** quoted in *Stevenson's Book of Quotations*

The only reason they say 'women and children first' is to test the strength of the lifeboats.

> **Compiler's great-grandmother**

Though every prospect pleases,
And only man is vile.

> **Reginald Haber**, Greenland's Icy
> Mountains'

Mirrors and copulation are abominable because they increase the number of men.

> **Jorge Luis Borges**

Let us love dogs; let us love only dogs!
Men and cats are unworthy creatures.

> **Maria Bashkirtseff**, quoted in *Macmillan
> Treasury of Revelant Quotations* (Edward F.
> Murphy)

There's nothing I enjoy more than being on stage and slagging men off.

> **Barbara Gogan**, quoted in *Woman Talk*
> (Michele Brown and Ann O'Connor)

Women's faults are many,
Men have only two:
Everything they say
And everything they do.

> Graffito in Liverpool ladies, quoted in
> *Graffiti: The Scrawl of the Wild* (Roger
> Kilroy)

When God invented men drivers she was only joking.

> Seen in the back of a car in Twickenham

PICKING ON MEN

A woman driver is one who drives in exactly the same way as a man driver and gets blamed for it.

> Quoted by Kenneth Edwards in *More Things I Wish I'd Said*

He: All feminists hate men. *She:* Don't be silly, you can't *hate* something so pathetic.

> Overheard on a bus

If you catch a man, throw him back.

> Women's Lib Slogan, Australia 1975 quoted in *Dictionary of Contemporary Quotations* (Jonathon Green)

One of the rarest things that a man ever does is to do the best he can.

> **Josh Billings,** quoted in *Macmillan Treasury of Relevant Quotations* (Edward F. Murphy)

To most men duty means something unpleasant which the other fellow ought to do.

> **George Horace Lorimer,** *Ibid.*

The only difference between men is the colour of their neckties.

> **Helen Broderick,** in *Top Hat,* quoted in *Movie Quote Book* (H. Haun)

A woman who strives to equal a man lacks ambition.

> **Anon**

Girls are called birds because they're always picking up worms.

> **Anon**

That all men should be brothers is the dream of people who have no brothers.

> **Charles Chincholles,** *Pensées de Tout le Monde*

All men are equal before fish.

Herbert Hoover

When a man is wrapped up in himself, he makes a pretty small package.

John Ruskin, quoted in *Quotations for Our Time* (Dr. Laurence Peter)

If It Happens To A Man It Must Be Serious.

Ms, November 1976

It is quite obvious that children are more beautiful than adults. Out of any ten children, seven or eight are delightful; whereas out of men . . .

Françoise Mallet-Joris, quoted in *Macmillan Treasury of Revelant Quotations* (Edward F. Murphy)

The man's a fool. Example of tautology.

Anon

Oh, well, you know men.

Editor's mother

2

MEN

Stages in Life of

MEN

Youth of

The parent who could see his boy as he really is would shake his head and say, 'Willie is no good, I'll sell him.'

Stephen Leacock, quoted in *Treasury of Humorous Quotations* (Esar)

A boy does not put his hand in his pocket until every other means of gaining his end has failed.

J. M. Barrie, *Sentimental Tommy*

A boy is, of all wild beasts, the most difficult to manage.

Plato

The God to whom little boys say their prayers has a face very like their mother's.

J. M. Barrie, quoted in *Who Said That?* (Renie Gee)

A youth with his first cigar makes himself sick; a youth with his first girl makes other people sick.

Mary Wilson Little, quoted in *The Wit of Women* (L. and M. Cowan)

Puerile: boyish, childish.

O.E.D.

MEN

Maturity of

Most men do not mature, they simply grow taller.

Leo Rosten

The four stages of man are infancy, childhood, adolescence and obsolescence.

Art Linkletter, *A Child's Garden of
Misinformation,* Bernard Geis, 1962

Men deal with life as children with their play, who first misuse, then cast their toys away.

William Cowper, quoted in *The Nuttall
Dictionary of Quotations* (James Wood)

The difference between men and boys is the price of their toys.

Liberace, quoted in *A Book of Quotes*
(Barbara Rowes), Dutton

Old boys have their playthings as well as young ones; the difference is only in the price.

Benjamin Franklin, quoted in *A Book of
Unusual Quotations* (Rudolph Flesch),
Cassell

PICKING ON MEN

No man is ever old enough to know better.

Holbrook Jackson, *Ladies' Home Journal*,
January 1950

Boys will be boys, and so will a lot of middle-aged men.

Frank McKinnley Hubbard, quoted in
Treasury of Humorous Quotations (Esar)

A boy becomes an adult three years before his parents think he does, and about two years after he thinks he does.

General Lewis B. Hershey, quoted in
International Thesaurus of Quotations
(Rhoda Thomas Tripp), Penguin

A Jewish man with parents alive is a fifteen year old boy, and will remain a fifteen year old boy until they die.

Philip Roth, *Portnoy's Complaint*

. . . men, unlike women, never mature but are 'little boys all their lives' . . . 'they get angry very easily, are bad losers, and know little about self-denial'.

Robert Shields, reviewing *Parents* magazine and quoting Theodore I.
Rubin, *Observer*, 17th October, 1976

I like men to behave like men—strong and childish.

Françoise Sagan

It never becomes completely clear to the male that he is not part of his mother, that he is he and she is she.

Valerie Solanas, *Scum Manifesto*,
Matriarchy Study Group

I blame Rousseau, myself. 'Man is born free', indeed! Man is *not* born free, he is born attached to his mother by a cord and is incapable of looking after himself for at least seven years (seventy in some cases).

Katharine Whitehorn, quoted in
Handbook of 20th Century Quotations (Frank S. Pepper)

Growing up does not mean to the American boy taking on the responsibilities and the trials of full sexual behaviour. Growing up means wearing long pants like his elder brother, driving a car, earning money, having a job, being his own boss, and taking a girl to the movies.

Margaret Mead, quoted in *A Book of Quotes* (Barbara Rowes), Dutton

At thirty man suspects himself a fool;
Knows it at forty, and reforms his plan;
At fifty chides his infamous delay,
Pushes his prudent purpose to resolve;
In all the magnanimity of thought
resolves; and re-resolves; then dies the same.

Edward Young, 'Night Thoughts'

She held
a child to her breast
and fed him
and
he became a man
She held
a man to her breast
and fed him
and
he became a child.

M. Lakshmi Gill, 'Woman'

A man's home may seem to be his castle on the outside, inside, it it more often his nursery.

Clare Boothe Luce, quoted in *A Book of Quotes* (Barbara Rowes), Dutton

PICKING ON MEN

I refuse to consign the whole male sex to the nursery, I insist on believing that some men are my equals.

Brigid Brophy, quoted in *Dictionary of Contemporary Quotations* (Jonathon Green)

MEN

Education of

The vanity of teaching often tempteth a man to forget he is a blockhead.

George Savile, First Marquess of Halifax,
quoted in *The Frank Muir Book*

The use of the birch is not to be deplored. All the best men in the country have been beaten, archbishops, bishops, even deans. Without sensible correction they could not be the men they are today.

Dean Ely, quoted in *Handbook of 20th Century Quotations* (Frank S. Pepper)

Show me the man who has enjoyed his schooldays and I will show you a bully and a bore.

Robert Morley, *Robert Morley: Responsible Gentleman*

His English education at one of the great public schools had preserved his intellect perfectly and permanently at the stage of boyhood.

G. K. Chesterton, *The Man Who Knew Too Much*

PICKING ON MEN

If you educate a man you educate a person, but if you educate a woman you educate a family.

Ruby Manikan, 'Sayings of the Week',
Observer, 30th March, 1947

Girls are better at passing school examinations than boys, according to the latest digest of GCE statistics published by the Joint Matriculation Board.

Guardian, February 3rd, 1970

A Man ought no more to value himself for being wiser than a Woman, if he owes his Advantage of a better Education, than he ought to boast of his Courage for beating a Man when his hands were bound.

Mary Astell, quoted in *The Female Eunuch*
(Germaine Greer)

You may lead an ass to knowledge, but you cannot make him think.

Ethel Watts Mumford, quoted in *The Wit of Women* (L. and M. Cowan)

MEN

As Bachelors

A bachelor never quite gets over the idea that he's a thing of beauty and a boy forever.

Helen Rowland

Bachelors begin at thirty-six. Up till this age they are regarded as single men. Most of them are very tidy, smell of mothballs, and have an obsessional old maid's fix about one of their ashtrays being moved an inch to the right.

Jilly Cooper, *Men and Supermen*

A bachelor gets tangled up with a lot of women in order to avoid getting tied up to one.

Helen Rowland, quoted in *Barlett's Unfamiliar Quotations* (Leonard Louis Levinson)

A bachelor who has passed forty is a remnant; there is no good material in him.

Helen Rowland, quoted in *The Wit of Women* (L. and M. Cowan)

Miss, n. A title with which we brand unmarried women to indicated that they are in the market. Miss, Missis (Mrs) and Mister (Mr) are the three most distinctly disagreeable words in the language, in sound and sense. Two are corruptions of Mistress, the other of Master . . . If we must have them, let us be consistent and give one to the unmarried man. I venture to suggest Mush, abbreviated to Mh.

Ambrose Bierce, *The Devil's Dictionary,*
Penguin

There certainly are not so many men of large fortune in the world, as there are pretty women to deserve them.

Jane Austen, *Mansfield Park*

There is nothing will kill a man so soon as having nobody to find fault with but himself.

George Eliot

MEN

As Prey

Men, being conditioned badly, are always feeling nooses closing around their necks, even dumpy boors no girl would take on a bet.

Cynthia Heimel, *Sex Tips For Girls*

Most men, no matter how old, arthritic and peevish, trot through life complacently believing that all women, no matter how young and desirable, are after them. Life to the average man is a jungle littered with man-traps, wedding rings and tigresses in miniskirts waiting to pounce. He flits through this jungle, twittering with relief every time he manages to escape (as he thinks) at worst marriage, and at best an expensive dinner.

Angela Ince, quoted in *The Wit of Women*
(L. and M. Cowan)

Very often it seems to me that middle-aged gentlemen overrate the attraction they have for younger women.

Joan Lester, MP, *Ibid.*

MEN

As Lovers

It's a pity you have to fall in love with boys because they always pinch you.

> **Beryl** (aged 7), quoted in *God Bless Love* (Nanette Newman)

In the spring a young man's fancy lightly turns—and turns—and turns.

> **Helen Rowland,** quoted in *Treasury of Humorous Quotations* (Esar)

Oh, is it, then, Utopian
To hope that I may meet a man
Who'll not relate, in accents suave,
The tales of girls he used to have.

> **Dorothy Parker,** 'De Profundis', *The Penguin Dorothy Parker*

The trouble is, Jane is still young enough to think one man may be better than another.

> **Jennie Lee,** quoted by Jill Craigie, *The Times,* 12th November, 1980

PICKING ON MEN

Many a young man who dreams of a blue-eyed blonde with a science degree is quite unaware that his deepest need is maybe for a woman whose chief talent is to worship him.

Professor Igor Kan, 'Sayings of the Week', *Observer*, 10th April, 1977

The man who worships the ground his girl walks on probably knows her father owns the property.

Dr. Laurence Peter, *Quotations for Our Time*

They always hold up something more than they're prepared to give.

Janis Joplin, interviewed on 'The Dick Cavett Show'

Before you meet your handsome prince you have to kiss a lot of toads.

Graffito, quoted in *Graffiti: The Scrawl of the Wild* (Roger Kilroy)

Love starts when you sink into his arms and ends with your arms in his sink.

Anon

Prince or commoner, tenor or bass,
Painter or plumber or never-do-well,
Do me a favour and shut your face—
Poets alone should kiss and tell.

Dorothy Parker, 'L'Envoi to Ballade of a Talked Off Ear'

Scratch a lover and find a fool.

Dorothy Parker, 'Enough Rope'

. . . the sort of fool who thinks a woman loves him just because he loves her.

Somerset Maugham, *The Constant Wife*

MEN, As Lovers

Oh, beggar or prince, no more, no more!
Be off and away with your strut and show.
The sweeter the apple, the blacker the core—
Scratch a lover, and find a foe!

> **Dorothy Parker**, 'L'Envoi to Ballade of
> Great Weariness'

Witholding intimacy is characteristic of many men, the secret
sex, ever holding back, controlling the intensity of the connec-
tion, not demonstrating the loving they feel.

> **Frances Lear**, 'Love Between Grown-
> Ups', *Ms*, December 1983

Most men make love as though they're all alone.

> **Dyan Sheldon**, *The Dreams of an Average Man*

The only thing that can make a woman feel lonelier than a vi-
brator can make her feel is a man.

> **Isha Elafi**

It takes two to make a love affair and a man's meat is too often
a woman's poison.

> **Somerset Maugham**, *The Summing Up*

Over and above
Everything else
Jeremy was in love with himself
But he didn't get on
Together.

> **William John Sircombe**, 'Pick of the
> 1970 "Look" Poems', *Sunday Times*, 20th
> December, 1970

Some men break your heart in two,
Some men fawn and flatter,

PICKING ON MEN

Some men never look at you;
And that cleans up the matter.

Dorothy Parker, 'Experience'

I had rather hear my dog bark at a crow than a man swear he loves me.

William Shakespeare, *Much Ado About Nothing*

Every man has a special place in his heart for one woman above all others, and also for one car.

Prince Michael of Kent, 'Sayings of the Week', *Observer*, 21st October, 1984

I cannot much wonder that men are always so liberal in making presents of their hearts. Let us consider the ingredients that make up the heart of a man. It is composed of dissimulation, self-love, vanity, inconstancy, equivocation, and such fine qualities.

Henrietta Howard, quoted in *The Wit of Women* (L. and M. Cowan)

Women in love are less ashamed than men. They have less to be ashamed of.

Ambrose Bierce, *The Cynic's Word Book*

. . . wooing, wedding, and repenting is as a Scotch jig, a meas-ure, and a cinque-pace: the first suit is hot and hasty, like a Scotch jig, and full as fantastical; the wedding, mannerly modest as a measure, full of state and ancientry; and then comes repentance and, with his bad legs, falls into the cinque-pace faster and faster, till he sinks into his grave.

William Shakespeare, *Much Ado About Nothing*

A man fifty-four years old who in his heart does not really be-lieve he is too old to fall in love needs all the help a tailor can give him.

Allan Seager, Introduction to *Memoirs of a Tourist* (Stendhal)

'When I open your letters,' wrote a woman to her lover, 'and see six pages covered with debates . . . and not a single word about ordinary life, I feel faint.' And, later, 'Now see how mean you are. I sense that every word concerning the most stupid business is twice, no ten, a hundred times more interesting to you than my pouring out my whole heart to you. Mention [work] and your eyes light up. Write about myself, that I'm tired, that I miss you and it's quite different.'

Rosa Luxemburg, quoted by Jill Tweedie, *Guardian*, 28th February, 1984

They hail you as their morning star
Because you are the way you are.
If you return the sentiment,
They'll try to make you different.

. . .

They'd alter all that they admired.
They make me sick, they make me tired.

Dorothy Parker, 'Men', *The Penguin Dorothy Parker*

Yet each man kills the thing he loves,
By each let this be heard,
Some do it with a bitter look,
Some with a flattering word.
The coward does it with a kiss,
The brave man with a sword.

Oscar Wilde, 'The Ballad of Reading Gaol'

MEN

Marriage to

The trouble with some women is they get all excited about nothing—and then marry him.

Cher Bono, 1982

Bigamy is having one husband too many. Monogamy is the same.

Quoted by **Erica Jong** in *Fear of Flying*

In olden times sacrifices were made at the altar—a practice which is still continued.

Helen Rowland, quoted in *Violets and Vinegar* (Jilly Cooper and Tom Hartman)

Seeing unhappiness in the marriage of friends, I was content to have chosen music and laughter as a substitute for a husband.

Elsa Maxwell, quoted in *The Wit of Women* (L. and M. Cowan)

Celibacy is the better stake, since the best husband is not worth a fig.

'Madame', *Ibid.*

PICKING ON MEN

I would rather be a beggar and single, than a Queen and married
. . . I should call the wedding ring the yoke-ring.

Elizabeth I, *Ibid.*

I would not marry God.

Maxine Elliott, cable when her
engagement was rumored, quoted in
Maxine (Diana Forbes Robertson)

I never married because there was no need. I have three pets at
home which answer the same purpose as a husband. I have a dog
which growls every morning, a parrot which swears all the after-
noon and a cat that comes home late at night.

Marie Corelli, quoted in *What the Doctor
Thought* (James Crichton-Browne)

Not till God made men of some other metal than earth [would I
marry]. Would it not grieve a woman to be overmastered with a
piece of valiant dust! to make an account of her life to a clod of
wayward marl?

William Shakespeare, *Much Ado About
Nothing*

How can a woman promise to honour and obey him whom she
feels to be her inferior? How can she condemn herself to daily,
hourly intercourse with one, who can neither increase her
knowledge, foster her virtues, nor even comprehend the capa-
bilities she may possess . . . ?

Mrs Hofland, *Fragments on Women,*
quoted in *Women Talk* (Michele Brown
and Ann O'Connor)

The men that women marry,
And why they marry them, will always be
A marvel and a mystery to the world.

Longfellow, 'Michael Angelo'

Even if a man was delightful, no woman would marry him if she knew what he was like.

A. C. Benson, *Paul the Minstrel and Other Stories*

I think it can be stated without denial that no man ever saw a man that he would be willing to marry if he were a woman.

George Gibbs, *How to Stay Married,* quoted in *Macmillan Treasury of Relevant Quotations* (Edward F. Murphy)

His designs were strictly honourable; that is, to rob a lady of her fortunes by way of marriage.

Henry Fielding, quoted in *Bartlett's Unfamiliar Quotations* (Leonard Louis Levinson)

A bridegroom: something used at weddings.

Anon

Girl: Do you think men should wear wedding rings?
Older woman: Definitely. Preferably through their noses.

Overheard on a bus

Women marry because they don't want to work.

Mary Garden, quoted in *Quotations for Our Time* (Dr. Laurence Peter)

When you see what some girls marry, you realize how they must hate to work for a living.

Helen Rowland, quoted in *The Wit of Women* (L. and M. Cowan)

Marrying a man is like buying something you've been admiring for a long time in a shop window. You may love it when you get it home; but it doesn't always go with everything else in the house.

Jean Kerr, *The Snake Has All the Lines*

147

PICKING ON MEN

A man is *so* in the way in the house.

> **Mrs Gaskell,** *Cranford*

When a girl marries she exchanges the attentions of many men for the inattention of one.

> **Helen Rowland,** quoted in *Violets and Vinegar* (Jilly Cooper and Tom Hartman)

Married men are viler than bachelors.

> **Sir Arthur Wing Pinero,** quoted in *Treasury of Humorous Quotations* (Esar)

There are some men in the world who behave with the greatest complaisance, civility and good nature to all ladies whatsoever; except one.

> **Anon** (early eighteenth century), quoted in *The Oxford Book of Aphorisms*

I married beneath me—all women do.

> **Nancy Astor,** speech at Oldham, 1951, quoted in *Handbook of 20th Century Quotations* (Frank S. Pepper)

You do have to pretend so much to make a marriage last.

> **Jill Bennett,** 'Sayings of the Week', *Observer,* 14th August, 1977

Marriage, indeed, may qualify the fury of his passion, but it very rarely mends a man's manners.

> **Congreve,** quoted in *The Nuttall Dictionary of Quotations* (James Wood)

In marriage, a man becomes slack and selfish, and undergoes a fatty degeneration of his moral being.

> **Robert Louis Stevenson,** *Virginibus Puerisque*

Never trust a husband too far, nor a bachelor too near.

Helen Rowland, quoted in *Violets and Vinegar* (Jilly Cooper and Tom Hartman)

Male domination has had some very unfortunate effects. It has made the most intimate of human relations, that of marriage, one of master and slave, instead of one between equal partners.

Bertrand Russell, quoted in *Quotations for Our Time* (Dr. Laurence Peter)

Some men feel that the only thing they owe the woman who marries them is a grudge.

Helen Rowland, quoted in *Treasury of Humorous Quotations* (Esar)

There's nothing in the world like the devotion of a married woman; it's a thing no married man knows anything about.

Oscar Wilde

A man needs a wife because sooner or later something is going to happen that he can't blame on the Government.

Anon

It is always incomprehensible to a man that a woman should ever refuse an offer of marriage.

Jane Austen, quoted in *Ms*, March 1983

Everyone ought to be leery of marriage. And every woman ought to be outright scared of it. (The cartoons of the confident bride and the trembling groom always seemed a terrible irony to me.)

Susan Starr Richards, 'How to Win At Marriage', *Ms*, March 1983

Retarded women make excellent wives.

Anon, letter to *Ms*, January 1973

PICKING ON MEN

There are two marriages in every marital union—his and hers. And, in the traditional marriage that is prevalent today, his is better than hers.

Jessie Bernard, *Ms*, December 1972

Margot is a good wife; she allows her husband to sap her energy and youth, and tax her good nature, and feels no resentment.

Fay Weldon, *Remember Me*

What better way to take the mystery out of a Mystery Man than to marry him?

Dale Messich, quoted in *Ms*, December 1975

Women are brought up to depend on men to sort out financial things . . . But we are getting more clued up. It's interesting how there is always one woman who asks how she can put money away without her husband knowing. That's when they all sit up and start scribbling furiously.

Susan Fieldman (solicitor running 'Money Matters'
seminar for women), interviewed by Maggie Drummond,
Sunday Times, 21st October, 1984

Clearly domestic murders present peculiar problems for the judicial process. What is less clear is whether our predominantly male judiciary are always as mindful as they might be of the 'provocations' caused to wives by their husbands.

Robin Lustig, *Observer*, 14th October, 1984

The occasional lacing of my husband's dinner with cat food has done wonders for my spirit.

Letter to the editor (name withheld!), *Ms*, December 1976

No man is a hero to his wife's psychiatrist.

Eric Berne, quoted in *A Book of Quotes*
(Barbara Rowes), Dutton

I have one case record of a man who claims he thought *he* was taking his wife to see the psychiatrist, not realizing until too late that his wife had made the arrangements.

> **Erving Goffman,** *Asylums,* quoted in *Macmillan Treasury of Relevant Quotations* (Edward F. Murphy)

. . . it is always the woman who must keep the thread straight, to save the marriage. Women choose for the family—though sometimes they must sacrifice themselves.

> **Sophia Loren,** interviewed by Geoffrey Wansell, *Sunday Telegraph,* 2nd September, 1984

The wives who are not deserted, but who have to feed and clothe and comfort and scold and advise, are the true objects of commiseration; wives whose existence is given over to a ceaseless vigil of cantankerous affection.

> **William McFee,** quoted in *Woman Talk* (Michele Brown and Ann O'Connor)

Powerful men often succeed through the help of their wives. Powerful women only succeed in spite of their husbands.

> **Lynda Lee-Potter,** *Daily Mail,* 16th May, 1984

Never feel remorse for what you have thought about your wife; she has thought much worse things about you.

> **Jean Rostand,** *Le Mariage*

When a man makes a woman his wife, it's the highest compliment he can pay her, and it's usually the last.

> **Helen Rowland,** quoted in *Treasury of Humorous Quotations* (Esar)

Having created a technological and social-structural juggernaut by which they are daily buffeted, men tend to use their wives as opiates to soften the impact of the forces they have set in motion against themselves.

Philip Slater, *The Pursuit of Loneliness*

My husband is a jolly good sort, one of those very hearty men. He wears plus-fours, smokes a long pipe, and talks about nothing but beer and Rugby football. My nerves won't stand much more of it.

A wife at Tottenham Police Court,
reported in the *Daily Mail,* quoted in *Violets and Vinegar* (Jilly Cooper and Tom Hartman)

In a husband, there is only a man; in a married woman, there is a man, a father, a mother, and a woman.

Honoré de Balzac, *Petty Troubles of Married Life*

The majority of husbands remind me of an orang-utan trying to play the violin.

Honoré de Balzac, quoted in *The Book of Unusual Quotations* (Rudolph Flesch), Cassell

This man, she reasons, as she looks at her husband, is a poor fish. But he is the nearest I can get to the big one that got away.

Nigel Dennis, quoted in *Woman Talk* (Michele Brown and Ann O'Connor)

The only good husbands stay bachelors; they're too considerate to get married.

Finley Peter Dunne, quoted in *Treasury of Humorous Quotations* (Esar)

One good husband is worth two good wives; for the scarcer things are, the more they are valued.

Benjamin Franklin, quoted in *Cassell's Book of Humorous Quotations*

A husband is a man who two minutes after his head touches the pillow is snoring like an overloaded omnibus.

Ogden Nash, *Marriage Lines*

Husbands are things that wives have to get used to putting up with.

Ogden Nash, *Ibid.*

You can't change a man, no-ways. By the time his Mummy turns him loose and he takes up with some innocent woman and marries her, he's what he is.

Marjorie Kinnan Rawlings, quoted in
Cassell's Book of Humorous Quotations

[Married men] are horribly tedious when they are good husbands, and abominably conceited when they are not.

Oscar Wilde, *A Woman of No Importance*

Chumps always make the best husbands. When you marry, Sally, grab a chump. Tap his head first, and if it rings solid, don't hesitate.

P. G. Wodehouse, *Adventures of Sally,* Barrie & Jenkins

The *divine right* of husbands, like the divine right of kings, may, it is hoped, in this enlightened age, be contested without danger.

Mary Wollstonecraft, *A Vindication of the
Rights of Women*

And fools are as like husbands as pilchards are to herrings, the husband's the bigger.

William Shakespeare, *Twelfth Night*

Don't think that every sad-eyed woman has loved and lost—she may have got him.

Anon

PICKING ON MEN

It is ridiculous to think you can spend your entire life with just one person. Three is about the right number. Yes, I imagine three husbands would do it.

Clare Boothe Luce, 'Sayings of the Week', *Observer*, 19th July, 1981

I think lots of men die of their wives and *thousands* of women die of their husbands.

J. B. Yeats, *Letter to His Son, W. B. Yeats, and Others*

MEN

As Fathers

Fathers should be neither seen nor heard; that is the only proper basis for family life.

Oscar Wilde

It is known that a father is necessary, but not how to identify him, except negatively.

Germaine Greer, *The Female Eunuch*

Human history, if you read it right, is the record of the efforts to tame Father . . . the greatest triumph of what we call civilization was the domestication of the human male.

Max Lerner, quoted in *Handbook of 20th Century Quotations* (Frank S. Pepper)

English history is all about men liking their fathers, and American history is all about men hating their fathers and trying to burn down everything they ever did.

Malcolm Bradbury, *Stepping Westward*

If necessity is the mother of invention, what was papa doing?

Ruth Weekly, quoted in *Quotations for Our Time* (Dr. Laurence Peter)

PICKING ON MEN

Men are generally more careful of the breed of their horses and dogs than of their children.

W. Penn, quoted in *The Nuttall Dictionary of Quotations* (James Wood)

How sad that men would base an entire civilization on the principle of paternity, upon legal ownership and presumed responsibility for children, and then never really get to know their sons and daughters very well.

Phyllis Chesler, *About Men,* Simon & Schuster, 1978

Unlike the male codfish, which, suddenly finding itself the parent of three and a half million little codfish, cheerfully resolves to love them all, the British aristocracy is apt to look with a somewhat jaundiced eye on its younger sons.

P. G. Wodehouse, *The Listener,* 30th May, 1963

Heredity is what a man believes in until his son begins to behave like a delinquent.

Presbyterian Life, quoted in *Quotations for Our Time* (Dr. Laurence Peter)

If it were natural for fathers to care for their sons, they would not need so many laws commanding them to do so.

Phyllis Chesler, *About Men,* Simon & Schuster, 1978

There are some extraordinary fathers who seem, during the whole course of their lives, to be giving their children reason for being consoled at their death.

La Bruyère, *Characters* (trans. Henri Van Laun)

. . . the problem of mental illness will never be solved while the male maintains control, because first, men have a vested interest in it—only females who have very few of their marbles will allow males the slightest bit of control over anything, and second, the male cannot admit to the role that fatherhood plays in causing mental illness.

Valerie Solanas, *Scum Manifesto*,
Matriarchy Study Group

When you've been afraid of a man like my father you're not afraid of God.

Theodore Fontane, *Effie Briest*, Penguin,
1967

The kind of man who thinks that helping with the dishes is beneath him will also think that helping with the baby is beneath him, and then he certainly is not going to be a very successful father.

Eleanor Roosevelt, *Ladies' Home Journal*,
December 1944

As fathers commonly go, it is seldom a misfortune to be fatherless; and considering the general run of sons, as seldom a misfortune to be childless.

Lord Chesterfield, quoted in *Treasury of
Humorous Quotations* (Esar)

Men want power over others—to revenge themselves on their fathers!

Irving Layton, 'Aphs', *The Whole Bloody
Bird: Obs, Aphs and Pomes*

MEN

As Adulterers

I have been so misused by chaste men with one wife
That I would live with satyrs all my life.

Anne Wickham, 'Ship Near Shoals'

The confirmed adulterer usually operates from a position of strength: 'I'm very much in love with Jennifer, you know. I wouldn't do anything to endanger my marriage, and little Gideon and Samantha mean everything to me.'

Jilly Cooper, *Men and Supermen,* Eyre Methuen

Husbands are chiefly good lovers when they are betraying their wives.

Marilyn Monroe

Lady, lady, should you meet
One whose ways are all discreet,
One who murmurs that his wife
Is the lodestar of his life,
One who keeps assuring you
That he never was untrue,

PICKING ON MEN

Never loved another one . . .
Lady, lady, better run!

Dorothy Parker, 'Social Note'

Eighty per cent of American men cheat in America—the rest cheat in Europe.

Jackie Mason, 1981

I don't know of any young man, black or white, who doesn't have a girl friend besides his wife. Some have four sneaking around.

Muhammad Ali, 'Sayings of the Week',
Observer, 28th September, 1975

I don't think there are any men who are faithful to their wives.

Jacqueline Kennedy Onassis

MEN

Divorce from

You never really know a man until you have divorced him.

> **Zsa Zsa Gabor,** quoted in *Handbook of
> 20th Century Quotations* (Frank S. Pepper)

He may be fat, stupid and old, but none the less he can condemn the woman's flabby body and menopause and encounter only sympathy if he exchanges her for a younger one.

> **Liv Ullmann,** extracts from *Changing*,
> quoted in *Observer*, 6th March, 1977

Oh, don't worry about Alan . . . Alan will always land on somebody's feet.

> **Dorothy Parker,** of her husband on the
> day their divorce became final, quoted in
> *Penguin Dictionary of Modern Quotations*
> (J. M. and M. J. Cohen)

I never hated a man enough to give his diamonds back.

> **Zsa Zsa Gabor**

PICKING ON MEN

The first time you buy a house you see how pretty the paint is and buy it. The second time you look to see if the basement has termites. It's the same with men.

Lupe Velez, quoted in *Woman Talk* (Michele Brown and Ann O'Connor)

MEN

Retirement of

When men reach their sixties and retire, they go to pieces. Women just go right on cooking.

Gail Sheehy, quoted in *A Book of Quotes*
(Barbara Rowes), Dutton

A man who has no office to go to—I don't care who he is—is a trial of which you can have no conception.

George Bernard Shaw, *The Irrational Knot*

Retirement means twice as much husband on half as much money.

Anon

MEN

Ageing of

Men can allow themselves to run to seed in the most appalling fashion. Women tolerate it because they think they're not entitled to ask for anything more.

Germaine Greer, *Observer*, July 1979

Every man desires to live long, but no man would be old.

Jonathan Swift, *Thoughts on Various Subjects*

There are no old men any more. *Playboy* and *Penthouse* have between them made an ideal of eternal adolescence, sunburnt and sauna'd with the grey dorianed out of it.

Peter Ustinov, *Dear Me*, Heinemann, 1977

Every man over forty is a scoundrel.

George Bernard Shaw, *Stray Sayings*

Men come of age at sixty, women at fifteen.

James Stephens, 'Sayings of the Week', *Observer*, 1st October, 1944

Men become old but they never become good.

Oscar Wilde

PICKING ON MEN

It seems the older men get, the younger their new wives get.

Elizabeth Taylor, quoted in *A Book of Quotes* (Barbara Rowes), Dutton

An old man is twice a child.

William Shakespeare, *Hamlet*

A man loses his illusions first, his teeth second, and his follies last.

Helen Rowland, quoted in *Treasury of Humorous Quotations* (Esar)

Men are not, of course, immune for fears of growing old, but their anxieties tend to focus on performance—in bed and on the job—rather than on appearance . . . they begin to worry at a much later age and state of decrepitude than women do.

Susan Jacoby, *Ms,* November 1983

Nowadays most women grow old gracefully, most men disgracefully.

Helen Rowland, quoted in *Treasury of Humorous Quotations* (Esar)

Men and cucumbers are worth nothing as soon as they are ripe.

Jean Paul, quoted in *The Nuttall Dictionary of Quotations* (James Wood)

Old men and comets have been reverenced for the same reason; their long beards and pretences to foretell events.

Jonathan Swift, *Thoughts on Various Subjects*

Old men are fond of giving good advice to console themselves for their inability to give bad examples.

François de la Rochefoucauld, quoted in *Treasury of Humorous Quotations* (Esar)

MEN, Ageing of

Many a man that can't direct you to a corner drugstore will get a respectful hearing when age has further impaired his mind.

Finley Peter Dunne, quoted in *Treasury of Humorous Quotations* (Esar)

MEN

Death of

It is easier to replace a dead man than a good picture.

George Bernard Shaw, *The Doctor's Dilemma*

The comfortable estate of widowhood is the only hope that keeps up a wife's spirits.

John Gay, *The Beggar's Opera*

. . . perhaps men should think twice before making widowhood our only path to power.

Gloria Steinem, *Outrageous Acts and Everyday Rebellions*

Where is the woman that would scruple to be a wife if she had it in her power to be a widow whenever she pleased?

John Gay, *The Beggar's Opera*

Men love death . . . In male culture, slow murder is the heart of eros.

Andrea Dworkin, quoted by Martin Amis interviewing Gloria Steinem, *Observer*, 15th April, 1984

PICKING ON MEN

What's the average man's life but a succession of automobiles? When he dies, we should carve on his tombstone simply the makes and years.

Richard J. Needham, *A Friend in Needham,* Macmillan, 1969

I haven't laughed so much since my husband died.

Anon, complimenting Victor Borge on his act, quoted in *Handbook of 20th Century Quotations* (Frank S. Pepper)

Index

Every attempt to include biographical material, where possible, has been made.

Index

Index

Index

Index

Index

Index